MONKEYS

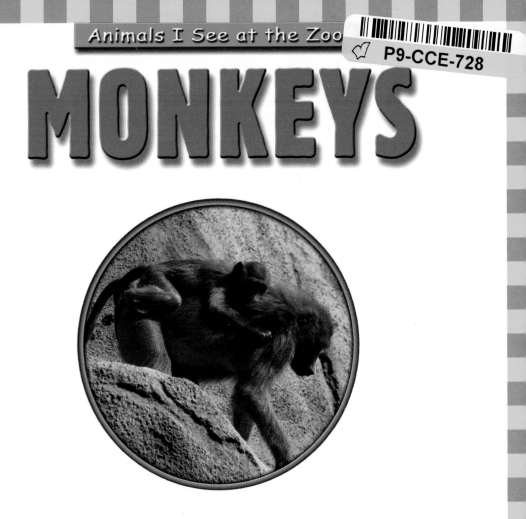

by JoAnn Early Macken

Reading consultant: Susan Nations, M.Ed., author/literacy coach/consultant

WEEKLY READER®

PUBLISHING

Please visit our web site at: **www.garethstevens.com**
For a free color catalog describing our list of high-quality books,
call 1-800-542-2595 (USA) or 1-800-387-3178 (Canada).
Our fax: 1-877-542-2596.

Library of Congress Cataloging-in-Publication Data

Macken, JoAnn Early, 1953-
    Monkeys / by JoAnn Early Macken.
        p. cm. — (Animals I see at the zoo)
    Summary: Photographs and simple text introduce the physical characteristics
and behavior of monkeys, one of many animals kept in zoos.
    Includes bibliographical references and index.
    ISBN-10: 0-8368-3272-8 – ISBN-13: 978-0-8368-3272-3 (lib. bdg.))
    ISBN-10: 0-8368-3285-X – ISBN-13: 978-0-8368-3285-3 (softcover)
    1. Monkeys—Juvenile literature. 2. Zoo animals—Juvenile literature. [1. Monkeys.
2. Zoo animals.] I. Title.
QL737.P9M2744   2002
599.8—dc21   2002016883

This North American edition first published in 2002 by
Weekly Reader Books
An imprint of Gareth Stevens Publishing
1 Reader's Digest Road
Pleasantville, NY 10570-7000 USA

Copyright © 2002 by Weekly Reader® Early Learning Library

Art direction: Tammy West
Production: Susan Ashley
Photo research: Diane Laska-Swanke
Graphic design: Katherine A. Goedheer

Photo credits: Cover © Ken Lucas/Visuals Unlimited; title, pp. 7, 17, 21 © William Muñoz; pp. 5, 19
© James P. Rowan; p. 9 © Gerald & Buff Corsi/Visuals Unlimited; p. 11 © Rick & Nora Bowers/Visuals
Unlimited; pp. 13, 15 © Joe McDonald/Visuals Unlimited

Printed in the United States of America

CPSIA Compliance Information: For further information contact Gareth Stevens, New York, New York at 1-800-542-2595

Note to Educators and Parents

Reading is such an exciting adventure for young children! They are beginning to integrate their oral language skills with written language. To encourage children along the path to early literacy, books must be colorful, engaging, and interesting; they should invite the young reader to explore both the print and the pictures.

Animals I See at the Zoo is a new series designed to help children read about twelve fascinating animals. In each book, young readers will learn interesting facts about the featured animal.

Each book is specially designed to support the young reader in the reading process. The familiar topics are appealing to young children and invite them to read — and re-read — again and again. The full-color photographs and enhanced text further support the student during the reading process.

In addition to serving as wonderful picture books in schools, libraries, homes, and other places where children learn to love reading, these books are specifically intended to be read within an instructional guided reading group. This small group setting allows beginning readers to work with a fluent adult model as they make meaning from the text. After children develop fluency with the text and content, the book can be read independently. Children and adults alike will find these books supportive, engaging, and fun!

— Susan Nations, M.Ed., author, literacy coach,
and consultant in literacy development

I like to go to
the zoo. I see
monkeys at
the zoo.

"Ooh, eek," monkeys whoop and shriek. It is fun to watch them play.

Monkeys have hands and feet like ours. They hold on to things with their hands and feet.

Monkeys swing on vines. They climb up in the trees.

Some monkeys look for food in the trees. They may eat leaves, flowers, insects, or fruit.

Some monkeys live in the trees. Some monkeys live on the ground.

Some monkeys
are small
and furry.

Some monkeys
are large
and fierce.

I like to see monkeys at the zoo. Do you?

Glossary

fierce — wild, cruel

shriek — to cry out in a loud, piercing way

vines — plants with long, thin stems

For More Information

Books

Arnold, Caroline. *Monkey*. New York: Morrow Junior Books, 1993.

Greenwood, Elinor. *Rain Forest*. New York: DK Publishing, 2001.

Shahan, Sherry. *Feeding Time at the Zoo*. New York: Random House, 2000.

Web Sites

Chaffee Zoo

www.chaffeezoo.org/zoo/animals/colobus.html
For a photo and facts about the colobus monkey
www.chaffeezoo.org/zoo/animals/macaque.html
For a photo and facts about the lion-tailed macaque

exZOOberance.com

www.exzooberance.com/virtual%20zoo/they%20walk/monkey/monkey.htm
For monkey photos and facts

Index

About the Author

JoAnn Early Macken is the author of a rhyming picture book, *Cats on Judy*, and *Animal Worlds*, a series of nonfiction picture books about animals and their habitats. Her poems have been published or accepted by *Ladybug*, *Spider*, *Highlights for Children*, and an anthology, *Stories from Where We Live: The Great Lakes*. A winner of the Barbara Juster Esbensen 2000 Poetry Teaching Award, she teaches poetry writing. She lives in Wisconsin with her husband and their two sons.

WAVES AND THE EAR

The three authors of this book work at the Bell Telephone Laboratories in fundamental research projects for finding and developing the most effective uses of new electronic devices.

WILLEM A. VAN BERGEIJK, 30 years old and a native of Holland, majored in biology as an undergraduate at the University of Utrecht. During his summer vacations he worked in the botanical and physiological departments of Philips Laboratories, Eindhoven, Holland. He also helped pay college expenses by making microscope demonstration slides for high school students. After his graduation he was a teaching assistant in comparative animal physiology at the University of Utrecht and became increasingly interested in zoology.

In 1953, Dr. van Bergeijk came to the United States to assist in research on the underwater hearing of frogs at the State University of Iowa. He earned his Ph.D. in zoology there in 1956. During the summers of 1953 and 1955 he held fellowships at the Woods Hole Marine Biological Laboratories and the Woods Hole Oceanographic Institution. Since December 1956, he has been associated with the visual and acoustics research staff at Bell Telephone Laboratories. Dr. van Bergeijk has written for both American and Dutch scientific journals.

DR. JOHN R. PIERCE was born in Des Moines, Iowa, in 1910. He studied physics at the California Institute of Technology both as an undergraduate and as a graduate student (Ph.D., *magna cum laude*, 1936). His boyhood interest in science came from reading the novels of H. G. Wells and Jules Verne, a pastime which has resulted from time to time in his publishing science fiction under the pseudonym of J. J. Coupling.

Dr. Pierce has made numerous notable contributions in the field of high-frequency electronics, microwave radar, and communications techniques. Reviewing his own career Dr. Pierce has said, "I find it difficult to locate any discovery or contribution that I regard as individually very important. Certainly the thing which is mentioned most by others is a rather simple way of designing electron guns for fairly large current densities, a procedure which leads to what has become known as a Pierce gun. I think that my most important discovery was that the traveling-wave tube, which Kompfner had already invented, was good for other things than those which he had in mind. Mainly, it seems to me I have been part of a new and more analytical approach in electronics which has grown up essentially since my college days."

Dr. Pierce is Director of Research—Electrical Communications, at Bell Telephone Laboratories. He is a member of the National Academy of Science, a Fellow of the American Physical Society and of the Institute of Radio Engineers, and has contributed articles to many publications, including the *Journal of Applied Physics*, the *Scientific American*, and the *Atlantic Monthly*. He is the author of *Theory and Design of Electron Beams*, *Traveling Wave Tubes*, *Electrons, Waves and Messages*, and, with Dr. Edward E. David, Jr., *Man's World of Sound*.

DR. EDWARD E. DAVID, JR., was born in Wilmington, North Carolina, in 1925 and received his bachelor's degree in electrical engineering with honors from the Georgia Institute of Technology in 1945. After service with the U. S. Navy as a fire-control officer, he pursued graduate studies at M.I.T., earning his Sc.D. in 1950. During this time he performed research on microwave tubes and noise theory at M.I.T.'s Research Laboratory of Electronics. In 1950 he joined Bell Telephone Laboratories, working in acoustics and underwater sound. He was appointed Engineer in Charge of Acoustics Research in 1956, studying the perception and coding of auditory information. More recently he was appointed Director of Visual and Acoustics Research. His articles have appeared in several publications, including the *Scientific American*.

WAVES
AND THE EAR

Willem A. van Bergeijk
John R. Pierce
and
Edward E. David, Jr.

SCIENCE
STUDY
SERIES

Published by
Anchor Books
Doubleday & Company, Inc.
Garden City, New York
1960

Available to secondary school
students and teachers through
Wesleyan University Press Incorporated
Columbus 16, Ohio

Some of the material in this book has been adapted from Chapters 2, 3, 7, 8, 9, and 13 of *Man's World of Sound*, John R. Pierce and Edward E. David, Jr. Reprinted by permission of Doubleday & Company, Inc.

Library of Congress Catalog Card Number 60–5948

THE SCIENCE STUDY SERIES

The Science Study Series offers to students and to the general public the writing of distinguished authors on the most stirring and fundamental topics of physics, from the smallest known particles to the whole universe. Some of the books tell of the role of physics in the world of man, his technology and civilization. Others are biographical in nature, telling the fascinating stories of the great discoverers and their discoveries. All the authors have been selected both for expertness in the fields they discuss and for ability to communicate their special knowledge and their own views in an interesting way. The primary purpose of these books is to provide a survey of physics within the grasp of the young student or the layman. Many of the books, it is hoped, will encourage the reader to make his own investigations of natural phenomena.

These books are published as part of a fresh approach to the teaching and study of physics. At the Massachusetts Institute of Technology during 1956 a group of physicists, high school teachers, journalists, apparatus designers, film producers, and other specialists organized the Physical Science Study Committee, now operating as a part of Educational Services Incorporated, Watertown, Massachusetts.

They pooled their knowledge and experience toward the design and creation of aids to the learning of physics. Initially their effort was supported by the National Science Foundation, which has continued to aid the program. The Ford Foundation, the Fund for the Advancement of Education, and the Alfred P. Sloan Foundation have also given support. The Committee is creating a textbook, an extensive film series, a laboratory guide, especially designed apparatus, and a teacher's source book for a new integrated secondary school physics program which is undergoing continuous evaluation with secondary school teachers.

The Series is guided by the Board of Editors of the Physical Science Study Committee, consisting of Paul F. Brandwein, the Conservation Foundation and Harcourt, Brace and Company; John H. Durston, Educational Services Incorporated; Francis L. Friedman, Massachusetts Institute of Technology; Samuel A. Goudsmit, Brookhaven National Laboratory; Bruce F. Kingsbury, Educational Services Incorporated; Philippe LeCorbeiller, Harvard University; Gerard Piel, *Scientific American;* and Herbert S. Zim, Simon and Schuster, Inc.

PREFACE

This is a small book on a subject about which numerous large books have been written. Such a drastic reduction cannot be made without penalty; either you sacrifice completeness or you lose lucidity, and all too often you wind up with an insufficient amount of both. In this little book we have tried to preserve clarity at all costs, and consequently the material is necessarily sketchy. Since we were forced to select, we took what we considered the most interesting and fascinating fragments of the vast fields of acoustics, anatomy, physiology, psychology, electronics, hydromechanics, zoology, linguistics, phonetics, and many other disciplines which have bearing on how the ear works. We hope that we will communicate the fascination which the ear holds for us, and that we may spark in the reader's mind some of the enthusiasm that inspired us in writing.

It may seem incongruous to find the personal pronoun "I" in a book on which three men have collaborated. We adopted this artifice for simplicity and to express the unity of our thought about experiences only one of us may have had.

Willem A. van Bergeijk
John R. Pierce
Edward E. David, Jr.

CONTENTS

CONTENTS

CHAPTER I

To Hear the World

When I think about hearing, I sometimes try to imagine what I would feel, what sort of person I would be, had I been born totally deaf. I would not be able to enjoy music or speech. Only with much and arduous training would I learn to speak coherently or, for that matter, to speak at all, unless someone somehow could convey to me by other means that there is such a thing as sound. It would be dangerous for me to venture out in the street, because I could not hear an approaching car nor the warning cry of a bystander. At least half of life would not exist for me, and the other half would be enormously complicated, even perilous.

Thoughts of this sort are rather sad and probably pointless, but they make you aware, in a negative way, of the functions of hearing. First of all, you realize that the ordinary world is full of sounds of enormous variety: the subdued babble of people in the next room, the hum of a fan, the whining buzz of a fly, the putt-putt of a lawn mower, and the whistle of a teakettle. As you see, all these sounds have different names: somehow they are distinguishable from one

13

another, so much so, indeed, that we even classify them by different names. But the hum of the attic fan is not the same as the hum of the table fan, nor does your mother's teakettle have the same whistle as your aunt's. And you know very well who is talking to whom in the next room. There are, therefore, smaller differences that distinguish sounds from one another, differences that do not merit classification by separate names. You can say that the attic fan has a louder hum, and that your aunt's teakettle has a higher pitch; you can say that the neighbor's lawn mower putt-putts faster than yours. But how do you describe the difference between Mary's and Lucy's voices? One may be somewhat harsher, or more nasal, or of higher pitch, but there remains that indescribable something that makes Mary sound uniquely herself. Of all the people you know, how many could you not immediately identify by their voices? I think you will find very few. It is remarkable that within the limitations of the human voice such a huge variety of small differences (so small that our best and most sensitive instruments sometimes cannot identify them) can exist. But it is even more baffling that the ear can distinguish among them, and that the brain, receiving signals from the ear, can recognize the particular differences quite readily.

The Meanings of Sounds

Let us see what else we can learn from common, everyday sounds. To learn something about the world, we must ask questions. For example: What do these sounds mean? Do they tell me anything? What do they do to me? Now obviously, a buzzing fly might irritate you to the point where you drop everything and set out to swat the pest. If it had not buzzed you quite probably would have paid it no mind. The lawn mower's putt-putt tells you that your neighbor has finally got around to cleaning up that dandelion jungle of his, while the teakettle informs you that the time has come for a coffee break. The hum of the fan tells you that it runs—so what? You can *feel* that anyhow.

So you see, the sounds you hear inform you of the state of the world around you, especially of that part of it which your other senses, such as touch and sight, cannot reach. Sounds inform you of the presence of a nuisance, of refreshment, of the disappearance of a nuisance (those —— dandelions!), or of something you feel quite indifferent about. They can arouse various emotions—anger at the fly, desire for coffee, or satisfaction that your hints finally got across to the man next door.

Of course I have selected my examples cleverly in order to demonstrate the various sorts of reactions sound may arouse in you. But you are undoubtedly aware that most of the sounds reaching your ears are of little or no importance. You simply do not listen to them. *Simply?* Is it really so simple to hear the sound that, for some reason, interests you amid a host of other, often louder, sounds? Most of us are familiar with the "party situation": a room full of people all talking, shouting, and even singing at the same time. Yet you can easily listen to a joke being told by someone on your right and the next moment "switch" to a couple of giggly girls behind you, without even moving your head. Your ears were getting the same sounds all the time, but you directed your attention now here, now there. If you had made a tape recording of the party with a single microphone at the spot where your head was, you would not be able to make any sense of the playback; you could not "direct" your attention anywhere but to the loudspeaker. The same sounds that were such fun to you at the party are now a garbled racket. Obviously *listening,* that is, concentrating on a particular sound, is not as "simple" as it seems.

So far I have talked exclusively about human hearing. Animals such as cats and dogs obviously have ears and just as obviously do hear with them. Birds have ears, although they are not easily visible from the outside; frogs have visible eardrums (as shown in Fig. 1.1), but where do you find ears in a fish? For

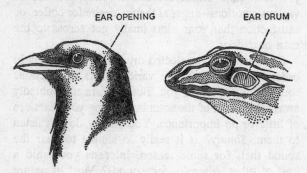

EAR OPENING   EAR DRUM

Fig. 1.1

that matter, how would you find out whether fishes have ears and can hear at all?

Before we jump into experimentation and discussion about these interesting questions, let us pursue a little further the same type of thinking that turned out to be so fruitful for our understanding of the meaning of sound to people. That is to say, let us try to find out—just by recalling our experiences with animals—what sounds they hear, how they react to them (you could say something about the "meaning" of a particular sound, if you should find that animals react to it in a particular way), and what uses animals make of their ability to hear. As you see, we are asking questions that may make us aware of the importance of sound in the animal's world. Obviously the world, or "environment," in which a particular animal happens to live, determines to a great extent what sounds are important to it. For instance, to a pet cat or dog the human voice is a very important sound and a welcome one at that. It is associated with food, shelter, caressing, and only occasionally with a scolding. But think of a wildcat; to him the human voice means only one thing—danger. On the other hand, the small noises of the forest mean dinner to the wildcat, while to the pet they may mean play.

Animal Messages

It is a striking thought that a creature hears its food, because in our own, human, perception we tend to associate smell and sight with the idea of sensing food; sounds play at best a very minor role. Yet many animals rely heavily on their hearing for a square meal, and some have no other means at all to obtain food. Have you ever observed a robin hunting for worms on a dewy lawn? Notice how he cocks his head and stands very still; then dashes forward, comes to an abrupt stop, and stands there again, head cocked, for a few seconds. He is not staring at anything, nor is he just behaving queerly. He is listening for the faint sound of a worm wiggling near the surface or coming out in the open. As soon as he hears one he starts looking for it and his head straightens, ready to snap up a juicy meal. Owls apparently hear the rustling of a mouse in the grass before they swoop down close enough to see the prey. But the most wonderful example of "hunting by ear" is provided by the bats. Bats are so specialized that they would starve to death if they should accidentally—or experimentally—lose their sense of hearing. The bat does not even rely on the noises its prey produces, as the robin and the owl do; instead it actively sounds them out, literally, by means of an acoustic sonar. I have illustrated this in Fig. 1.2.

The bat produces sounds of very high pitch, so high that the human ear cannot hear them (but the bat does hear them very well!). When there happens to be an insect—the exclusive diet of our most com-

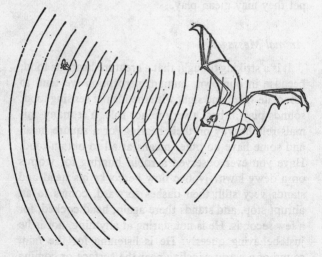

Fig. 1.2

mon bats—nearby, the sound waves bounce back from the insect and travel in reverse to the bat's ears. This *reflected sound* not only tells the bat that there is something edible around, it also tells him where it is, by a complex mechanism that makes use of the fact that the ear nearer the bug receives the reflected sounds first. Thus, in the drawing, the right ear of the bat gets the reflected sound waves before the left ear does. The bat then knows that the bug is somewhat to the right. Apart from the fact that bats hunt in the dark, where eyesight would not do them much good anyhow, they turn out to be indeed very nearly blind. So they are forced to use the same sonar technique to avoid obstacles and other dangers. But how does the bat know what is edible and should be pursued, and what is dangerous and should be avoided? Apparently sonar not only tells the bat about the presence and location of something, but also about its size, shape, and other properties. Professor Sven Dijkgraaf in the Netherlands succeeded in training some bats to distinguish between a small metal cross and a circle of the same surface area. So a bat hears the difference between a cross and a circle! It is simply impossible for us to imagine what the bat's world "sounds" like. Just think: All the things that we see with our eyes —obstacles, food, distances, relative speed of things, shape, size, and the innumerable other properties of our visible world—are represented in the bat's audible world. Small wonder, then, that many people, even the specialists on bats' sonar, often find themselves speaking of the bat's ability to "see with his ears," incongruous as it may seem.

Most of the sounds animals make, however, are not intended for such spectacular feats as the bat's radar.

But what are they intended for? We have seen so far that sounds inform animals and human beings about the outside world. (I distinguish between animals and human beings not for reasons zoological, but because we know about people firsthand and about animals only indirectly.) Either that world makes sounds spontaneously, so to say, or it reflects sounds, as in the case of the bats. Among the numerous things in the environment that could conceivably interest an animal are, of course, other individuals of the same species, especially those of opposite sex. The survival of the species depends on the animal's ability to find a mate. Now anybody can see that different species *look* different, and it is quite safe to assume the animals themselves see these differences too. A cat will not mistake a dog for another cat. But, as we have seen, the sense of hearing is really a "long-distance" sense; it becomes most important when the other senses—vision, smell, touch—cannot operate any longer because of obstructions or sheer remoteness from the thing to be sensed.

When a forest is densely populated with, say, a particular species of finch, it is quite probable that males and females meet each other by accidentally wandering within viewing distance. They never would have to utter a sound to make their positions known. On the other hand, finches establish *territory;* that is, each male "stakes out" a plot of forest, usually indicated by some natural markers such as odd trees, clearings, and so forth, but sometimes quite vague. This plot he considers his property, and he is determined to keep all intruders, especially other male finches, out of it. To make it known to all comers that they trespass at their own risk, he perches at the highest point in his domain and sings his characteristic "territory song." If our finch lived in a sparsely populated region he would have little need for insistence on his rights, since no other male would bother him. But by the same token he would have trouble meeting a female, unless he perched in a treetop again and sang a "come hither" song to make it known that a bachelor of means, solid citizen, with large home, offers security to unattached female—apply in person.

These examples illustrate the role of hearing in *communication*. One bird makes a sound which informs the other of the state of mind of the caller: he is determined to keep other male finches out, but is anxious to have girl finches come in. There is a real *message* in these calls—that is, a "personal" note. It does not just inform any listener of a bird's being there; it specifically tells all other finches that here sits one finch who has no use for other finches except females. You can think of many other examples, such as the clucking of the hen, which tells the chicks, "Mother has found food"; or the screeching of the blue jay, which informs other blue jays—and, incidentally, all sorts of other animals that have learned to heed the jay's noise—that he has seen danger approaching. It is this *sending and receiving of meaningful messages* which I will refer to as *communication*.

Codes and Communication

Obviously, animals and human beings make many sounds not intended as messages, although they carry information about the presence and even the feelings of the noisemaker. For instance, I may walk down the hall whistling a tune; I do not intend to make my presence or mood known to anybody, but whoever hears me knows I am there and probably in a good humor. This I do not consider communication. Conversely, a baby could be yelling his little head off, obviously trying to convey something to the parents; but they may be at a complete loss to know what the infant wants, unable to understand the message. Again no communication.

Communication does not always involve the production and perception of sounds. A great deal of communication goes on by means of the visual sense (the fang-flashing of a dog is a more eloquent sign of his intentions than any amount of growling); the sense of touch (a caress or kiss conveys far more than a long declaration of love); and even the sense of smell.

In most animals communication by sounds is extensively used for the expression of emotions: anger, fear, joy, satisfaction, the sex urge, and sociability have characteristic sounds associated with them. A dog snarls and growls when angry, yelps and whines when scared, barks or yips when happy. Cats purr when satisfied and make the most hideous racket during courtship.

In man we find some of the same characteristic sounds. We scream, groan, chuckle, sob, yell, and howl; you can easily identify the emotions expressed by these sounds. However, in the human being this basic system of communication is superseded by our ability to use sounds as building blocks in a *symbolic code* of communication which we call *language*. Not only can we express our basic emotions in this coded form, but we use it to express rational thoughts, even very abstract ideas. Some people argue that we can think rationally only because we have a language. This argument has a lot to recommend it; just try for yourself to think about something without "thinking in words," or perhaps in numbers, which are after all also a code. Of course, you must not think of emotional subjects such as a friend of the opposite sex— that I call "dreaming." But you will probably find it impossible to think about any prosaic subject, such as how you will spend the rest of the day or the rest of your money, without using words. For most people, as far as I am aware, thinking involves "talking to themselves."

Human languages are so very different from animal "languages" that the word communication takes on a new dimension when used to describe human language behavior. Although my definition of communication, a few pages back, as the sending and receiving of meaningful messages is still valid, the word "meaningful," which in the animal world embraced only a very limited number of sounds, describes a virtually limitless universe of message for people.

I have tried to give you an idea of the important role sounds and hearing play in the lives of men and animals: for orientation, the finding of food, the avoidance of danger, mating, communication. I have not even mentioned such things as music, scientific and military observation, and the other arts and activities in which the human ear is used. Some of these will be discussed in later chapters. First, however, we should examine what *sound* is; then we are equipped to inquire just what and how we hear, what goes on in that sensitive and versatile organ, the *ear,* and how the *brain* receives and interprets the nervous signals from the ear. Finally, we will have a somewhat closer look at a few of the interesting problems of acoustic orientation, communication, and the reproduction of sound.

As we go along, we shall have to ask numerous questions beginning with what? how? and why? I would like to quote what Georg von Békésy—in the opinion of many, the greatest living authority on the ear—has to say on the subject:

> . . . As I see it, the difference between successful and unsuccessful research is basically a problem of asking the right question. I can distinguish the following types of questions:
> 1. The unimportant question
> 2. The premature question
> 3. The strategic question
> 4. The stimulating question
> 5. The embarrassing question (the kind that is asked at meetings)
> 6. The pseudo-question (often a consequence of a different definition or a different approach)
>
> As a beginner I wanted to find a strategic question, but I was unable to do so. . . .

Békésy believes that stimulating questions are the most valuable kind: they induce you to *do* something. When you do things you may turn up strategic questions. They lead to Knowledge.

CHAPTER II

The Power of Sound

I have often wondered at the radio waves which flow through us, penetrating our bodies but not touching our senses. Somewhere within us electric and magnetic fields of minute power are all the time singing, exhorting, and perhaps calling for help. When the light of the sun falls on us we receive, all unaware, the same electromagnetic impulses that radio astronomers study. When we stand under the stars at night, we are exposed to electromagnetic signals from the suns and galaxies, some of which are not visible to our eyes. A sensitive radio set held in the hand will respond to the minute power of these radio waves; it will translate them into sound that we can hear. Yet, directly, our senses are unaware of the world of radio about us.

Perhaps it is this inaccessibility to the common senses of hearing and sight that lends wonder to these unheard signals. After all, light waves, like radio waves, are electromagnetic in nature. They too are ever present, except in the darkest caves made by nature or man, and they too tell us things of tremendous complexity and variety. If we are to wonder at the nature of things rather than at what is hidden from our senses, the world of light about us is as wonderful as the world of radio, but neither is more wonderful than the world of sound.

The minute radio signals surrounding us are no fainter than the sounds we hear clearly on a quiet night. To a living, thinking being who could not hear, faint sounds would be as strange and difficult to detect as are faint radio waves. While sound does not come to us from far galaxies as do radio waves and light, it does come to us from a multitude of private worlds of great complexity and interest—from the people with whom we speak each day. Indeed, the complexity of radio waves—the pattern in them which corresponds to spoken language—really pertains to the world of sound rather than to the world of radio. If the acts of speaking and hearing seem to us less wonderful than radio, it is surely because they are more familiar, and perhaps partly because they are less well understood. We find it difficult adequately to tell their wonders. Yet even if we do not fully understand the intricacies of the ear and are baffled to know in what manner the brain processes and comprehends the signals it receives, we have a very clear idea of the nature of sound waves in the air. We can measure their power. We know how they travel from one place to another. We can explain the patterns they form as they travel.

Any sort of motion generates sound—a violent explosion, the buzzing wings of a fly, the vibrations of cymbals struck together. Part of the energy of the motion goes into sound, which travels out in all directions, eventually striking walls, tables, chairs, and perhaps human ears. Yet, unless it is very loud, sound does not make walls or tables vibrate so that we can see or feel the motion, despite the fact that sight and touch are delicate senses. Moreover, sound made by the feeble power of a buzzing fly can be very loud on a hot, quiet summer day. We are able to hear very weak sounds indeed, and yet loud sounds are not as powerful as we might at first suppose. The faint sounds that we hear have powers almost inconceivably small in comparison with common phenomena, and even loud sounds have little power by other standards.

The Range of Sound Power

To form some estimate of the faintness of audible sounds, let us call up Marcus Vitruvius Pollio, a Roman architect who had a particular interest in theater acoustics. He pictured sound as a material flow going out in ever expanding spheres from its source; a particular sound flowing out as a one-foot sphere at one moment would an instant later have spread much more thinly to make a twelve-foot sphere of fainter sound.

When we are six feet from a loudly buzzing fly, the ear collects only a minute fraction of the sound the fly produces, about that associated with a fifth of a square inch of the total area of the surface of the sphere. When we are six feet away, the sphere of sound is twelve feet in diameter, and its surface has an area of 65,000 square inches. Thus, six feet from a buzzing, the sound we hear is 1/300,000 flypower. It is less than this, for not all the fly's power is used in producing sound.

We ordinarily reckon power in somewhat different terms. We are familiar with horsepower in connection with cars, and with the watt in connection with light bulbs. A 100-horsepower car seems feeble indeed in

27

these days. A 100-watt bulb is much less powerful; 100 watts is about an eighth of one horsepower. Yet those familiar with high-fidelity phonographs and radios will recognize that a 100-watt amplifier could rock the house. In fact, a 10-watt amplifier produces more sound than the average housewife will tolerate.

Imagine, now, that we conceive of 100 watts of sound going out in all directions, spreading itself in larger and larger spheres. At the very most, how far away could we hear such a sound? The answer is, about two thousand miles. It is perhaps difficult to form a conception of the faintness of a 100-watt light or of a 100-watt sound two thousand miles away, but this does give some idea both of the sensitivity of the human ear and of the feebleness of some of the sounds with which we deal in hearing.

As a matter of fact, the example of the 100-watt sound is misleading, for to a degree sound disappears as it travels. Its energy is lost in heating the air through which it moves. Sounds of higher pitch are used up more quickly than lower-pitched sounds, but in some hundreds of miles virtually all the sound turns into heat.

It is more realistic to compare sound sources of different powers when the sources are at the same distance from the ear. Here, however, we encounter numbers so fantastically small that we cannot relate them even to imagined experience.

At a distance of three feet from a source sending out in all directions, the sound produces a tickling sensation in our ears when the source has a power of 10 watts, and it becomes actually painful as the power of the source is raised to about 100 watts. Yet the sound can still be heard if the power of the source is lowered from this painful level by a factor of ten million million, and through this whole range we can make useful discriminations and comparisons concerning the intensities of sound.

Detecting Decibels

It has been known for many years that our senses have a particular way of dealing with this fantastic range of sound powers. In 1834 the German physicist E. H. Weber stated what has come to be known as Weber's law: that a stimulus must be increased by a constant fraction of its value to be just noticeably different. We shall see in Chapter IV that this is not strictly true, but it does help to put us on the right track.

If we were to compare the lengths of two sticks, we might line the sticks up at one end and see whether one stick extended beyond the other at the other end. In such a comparison we would expect that the difference that would be just noticeable to our eye would be a constant division of an inch, say ⅟₁₆ inch, or ⅛ inch, regardless of the lengths of the sticks. But if we looked at the sticks from a distance, we might expect that the just noticeable difference would instead be a constant ratio. One stick might have to be 5 per cent longer, say, than the other for you to detect a difference. If this were so, the stick just noticeably longer than a 10-inch stick would be 10½ inches long, while a stick just noticeably longer than a 40-inch stick would be 42 inches long.

Weber's law states that it is this latter, fractional difference that is important in distinguishing the magnitudes of stimuli such as sounds. Experiments show that the least distinguishable difference in intensity of a sound is far closer to a fraction of the sound's power than it is to a constant difference in power. Thus Weber's law is at least approximately true, and this favors a system of measuring sounds based on power ratios rather than power differences.

Gustav Theodor Fechner, physiologist, physicist, invalid, psychophysicist and experimental aesthetician, has been called the founder of psychophysics. His work is summed up in *Elemente der Psychophysik,* published in 1860. Fechner went beyond Weber and asserted that a sensation evoked by a stimulus increases by a constant amount whenever the stimulus is increased by a constant factor. For instance, Fechner's law would tell us that every time we double the intensity or power of a sound we increase the sensation of loudness by a constant amount. Fechner's law is often confused with Weber's law. Like Weber's law, however, it emphasized the importance of ratios rather than differences of sound powers or intensities.

We shall see in Chapter IV that it is possible to attach numbers to our judgment, or subjective sense, of loudness. As S. S. Stevens of Harvard Psychoacoustical Laboratory has pointed out, neither for sound nor other psychophysical phenomena do the numbers bear out Fechner's law; rather, over a wide range of sound intensity, when we increase the sound power or intensity about eight times, we double the sensation of loudness (rather than increasing it by a given amount, as predicted by Fechner's "law"). Similar relations hold for other sensations, such as vibration and electric shock.

Nonetheless, the fact that Fechner's law is no law at all as far as loudness goes does not detract from the importance of reckoning sound power in terms of ratios. We do in general judge the relative loudness of sounds in terms of ratios of powers rather than in terms of differences in powers. We judge one voice to be just noticeably louder than another, or twice as loud as another, and we will make very nearly the same judgment when the speakers are near and their voices seem loud as we will when they are distant and the voices seem faint. Thus a particular difference in power that is negligible in comparing two loud sounds can be tremendous in comparing two faint sounds.

This all makes it clear that we want to compare the ratios of powers of sounds. We do this by making comparisons of power or intensity in this manner. If one sound is 10 times as powerful as another, it is said to have a level of 10 decibels, or 10 db for short, with respect to the first sound. A sound 100 times more powerful than the first sound is said to be 20 db stronger than the first, and so on according to the following table:

Ratio of intensities or powers of two sounds	Relation between powers or intensities in decibels
1	0 db
10	10 db
100	20 db
1,000	30 db
10,000	40 db
100,000	50 db
1,000,000	60 db
.1	–10 db
.01	–20 db
200	23 db
400	26 db
600	27.8 db

31

We see that in simple cases the number of decibels divided by 10 is equal to the number of zeros following 1 in the ratio of the powers or intensities of the two sounds. In more complicated cases the relation in decibels is defined in a mathematically consistent manner. Technically, the number of decibels is ten times the logarithm to the base ten of the ratio of sound powers.

A Scale of Everyday Sounds

The intensities of sounds are ordinarily related to a standard intensity of a ten millionth of a billionth of a watt per square centimeter, an intensity just about at the threshold of hearing. If a sound level is 10 db above this, the sound power is 10 times as great, and so on. In this manner we can describe the tremendous range of intensities of the sounds we encounter.

At 0 db intensity we can barely hear a sound.

The rustle of leaves in a gentle breeze produces an intensity of 10 db. So does a quiet whisper five feet away.

An average whisper at a distance of four feet produces a level of 20 db. This is also the sound level in a quiet garden in London.

In a quiet London street in the evening, when there is no traffic, the sound level is 30 db.

The night noises in a city may have a level of around 40 db.

A quiet automobile some tens of feet away produces a sound level of around 50 db.

Average shopping in a department store produces a noise level of 60 db, and very busy traffic produces a sound level of 70 db. An ordinary conversation at a distance of three feet is carried out at a level of between 60 and 70 db, just between the noise of shopping and the noise of very busy traffic.

Very heavy traffic, including an elevated line, produces a sound level of 80 db. At the noisiest spot at Niagara Falls the sound level is between 80 and 90 db, and a pneumatic drill ten feet away also produces a sound level of 90 db.

A riveter thirty-five feet away produces a level of almost 100 db, and hammering on a steel plate two feet away produces a level of 115 db as does an airplane propeller at 1600 rpm only eighteen feet away. These sounds are almost at the threshold of feeling and pain.

If a high-fidelity phonograph radiated a sound power of 10 watts uniformly in all directions, at a distance of ten feet the intensity would be about 110 db, or just a little less than that of beating on a steel plate at a distance of two feet.

This range of sounds, extending from the rustle of leaves in a gentle breeze to beating on a steel plate two feet away, covers a range of power of over ten billion times. The total range of audible sound, from the barely perceptible to the actually painful, is some hundred to thousand times greater. It is with this tremendous range of sound intensities that we deal in the world of sound audible to the human ear. And still the most painfully loud sound is weak by our usual standards of power. The faintest sounds of which we are aware, tiny compared with the buzzing of a fly or the singing of a mosquito, are almost indescribably feeble.

CHAPTER III

Waves, Frequencies, and Resonators

When we look at the world about us we have a vivid sensation of things near and of things far, of walls or roads receding into the distance, of people walking toward us or away from us, and all this we see in striking contrasts of shade and color.

The things we see do exist in the world about us in a very real way. Yet a little reflection convinces most of us that the vivid sensation of sight exists within us. Somehow, from the signals that come to our eyes from remote objects, we form in our brain a wonderfully accurate map or model of the world about us. Yet all that goes into this representation of the external world we derive from the light waves that are emitted or reflected by external objects and that fall on our eyes. The representation of the world that sight can afford us is wholly dependent on, and rigidly limited by, the physical properties of light.

So it is with hearing. We associate the sound of a man's voice with the man before us; we do not sense it as existing in our head. We hear footsteps approaching or receding. The ax strikes the log with a characteristic sound as the blow falls. When we see paper torn, we both sense the sound and see the act at a point outside ourselves where the tearing takes place.

Yet here too we are dependent on a sort of map of the events of the external world—a map based on disturbances reaching our ears through the air as a result of events that happen some distance from us. Our very ability to hear is based on the physical phenomena of sound, and these phenomena set some unavoidable limitations to the sense of hearing. Our whole mechanism of speech is also dependent on the physical phenomena of sound; speech is intelligible only in physical terms. An understanding of these physical qualities of sound provides a firm vantage point from which we can survey the less certain, less well-understood phenomena of hearing, to accept or reject theories as they are or are not in accord with what we know must be true.

The previous chapter pointed out that sound involves the generation of some sort of disturbance carrying energy, and that this energy spreads out in all directions, so that at a distance the energy falling on each square inch of surface is less than it is near the source of the disturbance.

The Nature of Sound Waves

Experience tells us that vibrating objects produce sound. Experience also tells us that we can sense the distinct vibrating effect of a strong sound without using our ears: a loud voice or a radio or phonograph with the volume turned way up will cause papers or tables to tremble or vibrate appreciably to the touch. Clearly, from the evidence of our senses, vibration is accompanied by the production of sound, and our sense of touch convinces us that sounds produce vibrations.

But how is the energy of the sound conveyed from the vibrating source to the object which the sound causes to vibrate? If sound is a flow of power from one place to another, how does the power flow? A thrown ball, a stream of water, a flowing river carry energy from one point to another. Is sound perhaps a flow or current of atoms, as the Latin philosopher-poet Lucretius imagined?

If sound were a flow of particles or atoms, we would expect the particles of two different sounds occasionally to collide, especially if the sounds were very loud, and so consisted of dense clouds of atoms. If sound were a flow of the atoms of a gas or a fluid, we would expect one sound to displace or deflect another, but nothing of the sort happens. Extremely violent disturbances in the atmosphere, such as the shock waves which a supersonic aircraft or an explosion produces, do modify and interfere with one another. But within the general range of intensity associated with audible sounds—a range of intensity including weak sounds and sounds billions of times as powerful—sounds from two sources, or a sound and its echo, pass freely through one another, neither interfering with the other. This is a very remarkable feature of the propagation or travel of sound. And measurements show a further remarkable fact: sounds differing in power by millions or billions of times all travel from source to hearer with the same speed.

We recognize, in another field, that this is also true of light, for faint light travels with the same speed as intense light, and the beams of two flashlights cross in mid-air without any mutual interaction or scattering.

This wonderfully simple behavior of sound, and of light also, which is very puzzling when we come to think of it, is characteristic of wave motion of a particularly simple type—wave motion in accordance with what are called linear physical laws.

Sound is, of course, a sort of flow of power, a transfer of energy from place to place. An arrow, a current of water, a flowing river carry energy from one place to another. Sound is carried by the air about us, yet sound is not a flow of air from the speaker to the ear. Rather, sound is like the waves we see traveling along a field of grain in the wind, a movement now here, now farther along among the grain, while the stalks remain rooted to the ground. More nearly, sound is like small waves which travel along the surface of water, like the ripples which radiate from a stone thrown into a pond. Observation shows us that the radiating circles of ripples caused by throwing two stones into a pond pass through one another freely; the same thing can be observed very accurately in a *ripple tank* you may have used in school physics courses. This is just the independent behavior we observe in the sounds from two sources. The ripples are an agitation that moves progressively from place to place in the water without carrying the water with it. In a like manner the waves of a sound are an agitation of the air moving steadily forward through the air. The air does not move bodily from place to place with the sound, and the air can support many independent sound waves simultaneously.

37

Patterns of Pressure and Velocity

Just what sort of disturbance does the air undergo as the sound passes through it? The general nature of the disturbance is a minute forward-and-backward motion of the air in the direction in which the sound travels. In so moving, the air is compressed in some places and rarefied in others. The air tends to flow from the regions of higher pressure into regions of lower pressure. Once in motion, the air has momentum, just as does a gliding skater or a rolling car. It cannot stop without compressing the air ahead of it. So the sound travels along through the air, pressure producing velocity, and the slowing of the velocity producing pressure as the air again comes to rest. This velocity, the velocity of the air molecules, is not the same as the velocity of the sound traveling from one point to another through the air.

The exact pattern of pressure and velocity (of the air) depends on the exact nature of the sound. A sharp clap of the hands produces an impulse of short duration along the path of travel—a short disturbed region with undisturbed air ahead of and behind it. As it turns out, this is not the simplest sort of sound wave to deal with in trying to understand the properties of sound.

Instead, we usually consider waves of sound of a special sort, called *sinusoidal waves*. These are produced, for instance, when the cone of a radio or phonograph loudspeaker moves smoothly back and forth as if it were driven from a crankshaft, vibrating at a frequency of f complete oscillations a second, and with the sort of motion in the graph of Fig. 3.1. (A crankshaft and connecting rod actually produce a motion not quite, though very nearly, sinusoidal.) This sort of motion is familiar to us in the motion of a swing and in the oscillations of the pendulum of a clock. This particular variation of position (position of the cone of the speaker in our illustration) with time, a *sinusoidal* or *sine wave,* is not just any smooth wiggly curve. It is a curve with particular mathematical properties that are important to us. The curve expresses, for instance, exactly how the height of the crank handle on a crankshaft rotating at a constant speed varies with time.

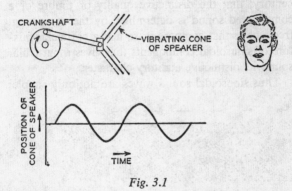

Fig. 3.1

It surprised physicists of the early nineteenth century when the French mathematician Joseph Fourier, a friend of Napoleon, proved a theorem showing that any motion—and this includes the motion of a speaker diaphragm—can be represented as a sum of sinusoidal motions of different frequencies and amplitudes, each of which is known as a component. This mathematical theorem is of great practical importance in dealing with sound. As we have seen, the independence of sound waves assures us that each sinusoidal component of motion will produce a sinusoidal sound wave which can be regarded as traveling independently of every other component sinusoidal wave of different frequency. Thus, however complicated the motion producing the sound may be, we can, in calculation or in speculation, regard the total sound as consisting of many independent non-interacting sinusoidal sound waves, each behaving just as if it were produced by itself, as if it traveled alone. In accord with this, the German physicist Hermann von Helmholtz showed, in the later nineteenth century, that the distinctive quality or timbre of a complicated sound is determined by the component frequencies that compose it; so it is a particular mixture of sinusoidal components that gives a particular sound its distinctive auditory character.

Thus sinusoidal sound waves are not only simple;

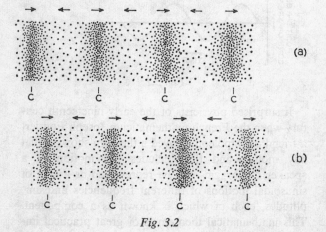

Fig. 3.2

they are extremely important as well. Let us, then, try to visualize clearly what happens when the sound from a sinusoidally vibrating source passes through the air from left to right. This is illustrated in Fig. 3.2. The little dots stand for molecules of air. Of course, there are actually many more molecules than are shown in the drawing. There are about four hundred billion billion molecules in a cubic inch of air. Moreover, these molecules are rushing to and fro madly, continually bumping into one another. What we have in Fig. 3.2 are two symbolic snapshots, that in *b* taken a little later than that in *a*. The evenly spaced points at which the molecules are pushed closest together, or the crests of the sound wave, are marked *C*. The little arrows above the crests indicate that at the crests the molecules are on the average moving to the right, the direction in which the sound travels, while midway between the crests the molecules are on the average moving to the left. Thus, as the wave moves past a fixed point, the velocity of the air molecules will be alternately to the right and then to the left. A periodic variation of forward and backward velocity of the air molecules is characteristic of a sound wave, just as is the periodic variation of density as crests and troughs pass us alternately.

Molecules in Motion

But what causes this motion of crests and troughs? By noting where the molecules are traveling toward one another and where they are traveling away from one another (that is, where the arrows point toward one another and where they point away from one

41

another), we see that as time passes the molecules will become bunched together just to the right of each crest, and they will become spread apart just to the left of each crest. The density of molecules will increase to the right of each crest and diminish to the left. This is just what has happened in going from time *a* to time *b;* and as a consequence each crest has moved a little to the right.

We also see in *a* that the higher pressure at each crest tends to push the molecules on the right of the crest to the right, and the molecules to the left of the crest to the left. Consequently the velocity of the molecules increases to the right of each crest and diminishes to the left of each crest. In *b* the molecules forming the new crest have acquired the same velocity to the right that the molecules of the old crest in *a* had, while the molecules at the position of the old crest in *a* have now lost some of their speed. Later these molecules will form a trough, with a velocity to the left.

Through this progressive process the sound wave travels through the air from left to right. At the crest, where the density and pressure are higher than average, the molecules always move to the right in the direction in which the wave travels, and they move to the left where the density and pressure are lower than average.

When we push a car, a gocart, or any other moving object, we do work—we expend energy. The harder we push on the moving object, the more work we do per second. The faster the object moves, the more work we do per second. The rate at which work is done is proportional both to force and to velocity.

Power is defined as the amount of work done per second. Hence, one expression for the power or energy flow through a square-centimeter area of the traveling sound wave is pressure times velocity. The power per square centimeter in a sinusoidal sound wave such as we have been discussing is proportional to the pressure caused by the sound wave times the velocity given to the molecules by the wave.

If sound waves were a truly linear phenomenon, two sound waves traveling through the air at once would not affect one another at all. At any point in the air the total pressure, the total density, and the total velocity of the molecules would be simply the sum of the pressures, densities, and velocities for the two waves traveling separately. For each wave the density, pressure, and velocity associated with that wave would satisfy the same mathematical relation or equation, a sort of equation called a linear differential equation, either in the presence or the absence of one or more other waves.

Sound waves, and the differential equations that describe them, are not exactly linear. But for sounds spanning the range of power from barely audible to painful, the waves are so nearly linear that we will make little error in regarding them as completely linear.

For a linear sound wave, the velocity would be proportional to the pressure. So if we increase the intensity of a sound wave enough to double the pressure, we double the velocity also, and the power becomes four times as great. We see that the power of a sound wave is proportional to the square of the pressure. It is also proportional to the square of the velocity. This means that the power range of a million million, which characterizes audible sound, corresponds to a pressure range of a million and also to a velocity range of a million. For the strongest sounds, the velocity and the pressure are both a million times as great as for the weakest sounds, yet the weakest sound can pass undisturbed through the strongest.

We can draw a useful symbolic picture of a sound wave in graphic form, as shown in Fig. 3.3. Here we

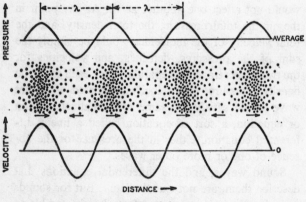

Fig. 3.3

have in the center the representation of Fig. 3.2: dots crowded together at the crests where the air is densest and dispersed at the troughs where it is least dense; together with arrows showing a velocity to the right, in the direction of travel, at the crests; and arrows to the left, contrary to the direction of travel, at the troughs. Above and below we have graphs or curves. The upper curve shows how pressure varies with distance, above and below average, at a given time. The lower curve shows how velocity varies, above zero (that is, molecules moving to the right) and below zero (that is, molecules moving to the left) with distance. We should note and remember that the pressure is greatest where the velocity of the molecules is greatest in the direction of travel of the sound.

In Fig. 3.3 the distance between crests has been indicated by the Greek letter λ (lambda). This is the wavelength. The wavelength may be measured in any units—feet, or inches, or centimeters.

Wavelength and Frequency

The velocity or speed with which sound waves travel through the air increases with temperature, but it does not vary with atmospheric pressure. For a given temperature it is the same for all altitudes, but, unlike men, it travels faster the hotter the day is. At a given temperature the velocity of sound is higher in a gas of low molecular weight, such as hydrogen or helium, than in a gas of higher molecular weight, such as nitrogen or oxygen. For reasons that will become apparent later this causes people to speak with a squeak if they breathe in helium rather than air.

For air at room temperature, the velocity of sound is about 1130 feet per second. As the wave travels past us moving to the right, crests will successively pass us at this speed. Suppose we measure the wavelength λ in feet. Then, as the wave travels to the right, the time T which elapses between the instant one wave crest passes a given point and the time the next arrives at this point is clearly

$$T = \frac{\lambda}{1130}$$

Since one complete cycle—crest, trough, and crest—passes each T seconds, the number f of crests passing in a second is

$$f = \frac{1}{T} = \frac{1130}{\lambda}$$

The quantity f, as we have noted, is the frequency of the sinusoidal sound wave. Wave crests pass a given point with the frequency f. Frequency is measured in cycles per second. A cycle is a complete change from crest, through trough, to crest again. We should notice that as the sinusoidal pattern of pressure and velocity constituting the sound wave travels past us, the pressure and velocity which we observe at a fixed point will vary sinusoidally with time at this frequency f.

The frequency of a sound wave is, of course, set by the frequency of vibration of the source of the sound—by how many times the vibrating source moves back and forth in a second. Thus the frequency is in a sense the primary quantity, and it is useful to express the wavelength in terms of the frequency. To do this we rewrite our relation between frequency and wavelength as

$$\lambda = \frac{1130}{f}$$

Frequency is no mathematical abstraction. In familiar terms frequency is associated with the characteristic we recognize as the pitch of a note. The table below gives the frequency and the wavelength for some octaves above and below middle C.

Octaves above or below (−) middle C	Frequency cycles per second	Wave length, ft.
−2 (C$_2$)	65.5	17.26
−1 (C$_3$)	131	8.63
0 (C$_4$)	262	4.31
1 (C$_5$)	524	2.15
2 (C$_6$)	1048	1.08
3 (C$_7$)	2096	.54
4 (C$_8$)	4192	.27
5 (C$_9$)	8384	.14

We see that sound waves are of a comfortable length. They are neither too long nor too short, and so we can form a clear concept of them. They have sizes corresponding to those of ordinary objects around us. This fact is important in determining the behavior of sound waves in ordinary surroundings.

Waves of light are about two millionths of a foot long—inconceivably shorter than commonplace objects. We know from experience that light travels in straight lines and casts sharp shadows.

The long rollers of the ocean are many feet in wavelength. They will flow right around a pile sticking up out of the water and are little affected by it.

These examples illustrate an extremely important fact about waves. Waves, whether of light, of the ocean, or of sound, are strongly affected by objects that are large compared with their wavelength. Among such objects they cast shadows and, indeed, appear to travel in straight lines. But waves are little affected by objects that are small compared with the wavelength. They flow around such objects. Sound

47

waves are betwixt and between as far as ordinary objects are concerned. In general they exhibit a mixed behavior. Thus, when a person sings a low note the sound is almost as strong behind him as in front of him, while if he whistles a high note the sound is appreciably stronger in front of him than behind him. Similarly, the low notes from a hi-fi speaker spread out in all directions, whatever the construction of the speaker, while the hi-fi enthusiast must take special precautions to make the high notes spread. Moreover, if we go around a corner from the speaker the very high notes will be all but lost.

Interference of Sound Waves

We have noted that two sound waves do not affect or distort one another as they travel through the same space. However, the ear is sensitive to the total sound pressure. If two sound sources with the same frequency are present at different locations, in some places wave crests will arrive from the two sources at the same time, and at such locations the pressure will be greater for the two sources than for either source separately. In other places, where we are a little nearer to one source than to the other, a wave crest will arrive from one source just as a trough arrives from the other. Then the sound pressure from the two sources together will be less than the pressure caused by the louder source alone. If the pressures from the two sources are equal, the pressure of a crest from one source and a trough from another source can actually be zero. At such a point the ear hears no sound.

Suppose that the cones of two speakers vibrate so

that they always move forward together and always move backward together. They are then said to vibrate in synchronism; their vibrations are synchronous and they form two synchronous sources of sound. Such an arrangement is shown in Fig. 3.4.

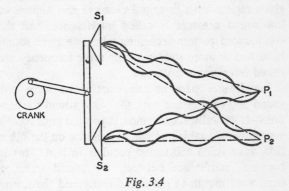

Fig. 3.4

Here cones S_1 and S_2 are clamped together by a bar and driven back and forth in synchronism by the same crank.

The sine waves proceeding from S_1 and S_2 to points P_1 and P_2 in Fig. 3.4 represent instantaneous snapshots of the pressure of sound waves traveling from the speakers to these two points. We see that P_1 is equidistant (three wavelengths distant, in fact) from both of the synchronous sound sources S_1 and S_2. Thus, at point P_1, the sound waves add, crest to crest and trough to trough.

Point P_2, however, is three and one fourth wavelengths from source S_1 and only two and three fourths wavelengths from source S_2. Thus, just when a wave crest arrives at P_2 from S_1, a trough arrives from S_2. Hence the net sound pressure of the two independent

49

waves from S_1 and S_2 is quite small at point P_2. Such cancellation will occur at any point which is an odd whole number of half wavelengths farther from one synchronous source than it is from another.

The addition of the pressures of sound sources to given regions of high sound pressure and regions of low sound pressure is called interference, and the complicated patterns resulting when we have sound from two or more sources of the same frequency are called *interference patterns*.

Interference patterns can exist if we have one sound source together with the same sound's reflections—from walls, for instance. If you put your mouth very close to a table and talk to a person on the other side, your voice will sound peculiar to him. This is because interference between the sound traveling from your mouth to his ears directly and the sound reflected to his ears from the table top prevents his hearing some of the higher frequencies of your voice.

When a person talks or a radio operates in an ordinary, hard-walled room, the sound reflected, and reflected repeatedly, from the walls forms, together with the direct sound, a very complicated interference pattern, which is different for different frequencies. Thus, some frequencies reach the ear much more strongly than do frequencies only a little different. We are used to this, and to the degree that it is found in ordinary rooms, it does not impair the quality of music or the intelligibility of speech. But in an ordinary room it does make it impossible to measure the frequency response of a radio or phonograph speaker (that is, how much sound the speaker puts out for a given power as the frequency is varied). Such measurements have to be made in a room with special sound-absorbing walls, a room called an *anechoic* (echoless) chamber.

The simplest form of interference between sound waves is that between a wave from a source and a reflection traveling back along the same path. A sound traveling down a tube or pipe and reflected from a plug at the end is an example.

We remember that a traveling sound wave has both pressure and velocity. Where the pressure is highest, the velocity of the molecules is in the direction of the wave's travel. Thus at the high-pressure point the velocity of the molecules will be to the right for a wave traveling to the right and to the left for a wave traveling to the left. We can discuss the reflection of waves in terms of either velocity or pressure. The ear is sensitive to pressure rather than to velocity, and we more often speak of sound pressure than of velocity (of the molecules). In some ways, however, it is simpler to discuss reflection in terms of velocity, and we shall do so here.

Reflections and Resonators

Let us return, then, to the reflection of a sound from a plug at the end of a pipe. At the plug the total velocity—the sum of the velocities of the incident wave (that is, of the wave striking the plug) and of the reflected wave—must be zero, since the air obviously cannot move right at the plug. If at the plug the velocity of the incident wave is positive (to the right), its pressure will be positive (greater than average pressure). The velocity of the reflected, leftward-traveling wave must be negative (to the left), and, because this is a leftward-traveling wave, the associated pressure must be positive. Thus, at the plug the velocities of the incident and reflected waves must cancel, and their pressures add, to give twice the pressure of the incident wave alone.

The velocity in a reflected sound wave is illustrated in Fig. 3.5. At the left the solid sine wave shows the

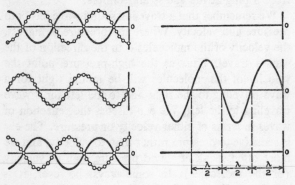

Fig. 3.5

velocity pattern of the incident wave, traveling from left to right toward the point of reflection. The velocity of the reflected wave traveling to the left is represented by a series of dots. To the right we have the total velocity, the sum of the solid and dotted curves. From top to bottom we see the velocity at three successive times.

We see that the total velocity is always zero at the point of reflection as indeed it must be, since at the plug the air molecules cannot move. The total velocity is also zero at points a half wavelength ($\lambda/2$) to the left, two half wavelengths to the left, etc. At these points the total pressure oscillates sinusoidally from high to low to high again, continually, at the frequency of the wave. Intermediate between these points the velocity is greatest, and it changes sinusoidally with time.

If we close a tube at both ends, the wave reflected from the right end will be reflected in turn from the left end and will combine with the wave already traveling to the right. If the wavelength is correctly related to the length of the tube, this doubly reflected wave will reinforce the incident wave, crest adding to crest and trough to trough. Such conditions are illustrated in Fig. 3.6. At the top is a closed pipe of length

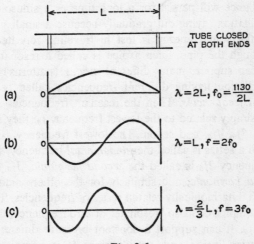

Fig. 3.6

L. At a we have a wave of length $\lambda = 2L$ reflected so as to reinforce itself. Here the frequency f_0 is *1130/2L*. For the pattern shown at b, $\lambda = L$ and the frequency is $2f_0$. For that at c, $\lambda = \frac{2}{3}L$ and the frequency is $3f_0$.

53

It is interesting to note that the frequencies associated with the patterns are all proportional to the velocity of sound and therefore would all be higher if the pipe were filled with a light gas such as hydrogen or helium rather than with air. We shall see that the vocal tract is a pipe-shaped structure, which likewise has certain frequencies associated with it. If we breathe in helium rather than air the frequencies are higher and we speak with a squeak.

If the air in the pipe is excited in any of the patterns a–c of Fig. 3.6, or in any other similar pattern of shorter wavelength and higher frequency, the disturbance will persist for a long time as a sinusoidal oscillation, dying out gradually because a small part of the sound energy is lost in traveling repeatedly through the pipe. Such a pipe is called a resonator. It can support many different *modes* (patterns) of oscillation having different frequencies called *resonant frequencies*. Then the resonant frequencies are all simply related to the lowest frequency f_0; they are $2f_0$, $3f_0$, $4f_0$, and so on. The lowest frequency f_0 of such a series is called the *fundamental* frequency, the frequency $2f_0$ is called the *second harmonic,* $3f_0$ the *third harmonic,* and similarly for the others among such a harmonically related series of frequencies. The closed pipe can also "resonate" at zero frequency, that is $0f_0$. It can support a constant pressure difference between inside and outside since it is completely closed. This fact will be important later when we consider partially closed tubes.

Resonators can be of many forms. The human vocal tract is a resonator. Fig. 3.7 illustrates schematically another common form of resonator—the pipe of a pipe organ. When a long tube is open at one end,

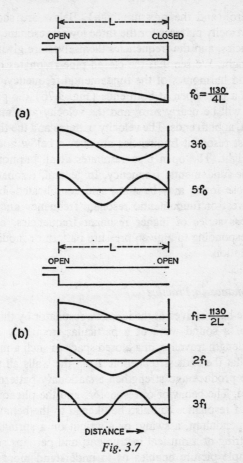

(a)

$$f_0 = \frac{1130}{4L}$$

$3f_0$

$5f_0$

(b)

$$f_1 = \frac{1130}{2L}$$

$2f_1$

$3f_1$

DISTANCE ⟶

Fig. 3.7

the velocity inside it will be nearly at a maximum (and the pressure nearly zero) at the open end. In *a* of Fig. 3.7 we have a closed pipe, which is open at the left, where the air blast from the wind chest strikes, but closed at the right end, so that there the velocity

55

is zero (and the pressure high). Below are shown the velocity patterns for the three lowest resonant frequencies, and the frequencies themselves are given to the right. We see that the closed pipe resonates only at odd harmonics of the fundamental frequency.

In a pipe open at both ends (Fig. 3.7b) the pressure will be nearly zero, and the velocity at a maximum, at both ends. The velocity patterns and the three lowest resonant frequencies are shown below and to the right. The open pipe resonates at all harmonics of the fundamental frequency. In general, resonators —whose forms may be many and complicated—have a lowest or fundamental resonant frequency and an endless series of higher resonant frequencies, each corresponding to a given pressure pattern or mode of oscillation.

Resonance in Practice

We have arrived at the idea of a resonator by thinking of a sound wave of a particular frequency and wavelength traveling in a closed space in such a manner that the endless reflections from the walls all add up to produce and strengthen a stationary pattern of sound. The behavior of resonators and the phenomenon of resonance can also be likened to the behavior of a pendulum, a swing, or a weight on a spring, or the string of a musical instrument; and perhaps such a simple picture enables us to understand more directly the pulsations of the air which occur in any resonator.

Consider the pipe at the top of Fig. 3.8, which is closed at the left end and open at the right end, and in which the air oscillates with the pressure pattern

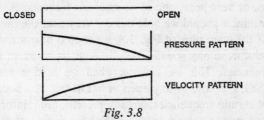

Fig. 3.8

shown below. At one instant the pressure will be high at the left end of the pipe, tapering to zero at the open end at the right. This causes the air to flow to the right and out of the pipe, gradually gaining speed. Soon the pressure is equal all along the pipe, but the air is rushing out of the mouth to the right. The air cannot stop suddenly; it keeps rushing out, and soon the pressure at the left is lower than atmospheric pressure and the velocity is zero. Then the air rushes in, moving to the left, and so on. There is a cyclic oscillation, sometimes with pressure and no velocity, and sometimes with velocity and no pressure. In between we have both pressure and velocity. Thus both pressure and velocity vary sinusoidally with time, but one is zero when the other is greatest. This is just like the oscillation of a spring supporting a weight: at certain moments the spring is compressed or stretched a maximum amount, with the weight momentarily at rest; while at times in between the weight is moving up or down but the spring has its normal length.

If we repeatedly push the weight-and-spring combination at just the right times, we easily set it in violent motion. An exactly analogous case is that of gradually "pumping up" on a swing. Similarly, the air in an acoustic resonator is easily set strongly in motion by a sound wave whose frequency is the same

57

as, or very near, one of its resonant frequencies. For instance, should we hold our ear very near the mouth of the open pipe of Fig. 3.8, we should hear strongly reinforced any sounds that are near its resonant frequencies. This we observe when we hold a conch shell, a bottle, or any open vessel to our ear. Sounds of certain frequencies, already present, are reinforced and made to stand out from the background of other sounds.

In the early days of acoustics this was the only means for sorting out sounds of different frequencies —that is, for analyzing sounds. In analyzing complex sounds, Helmholtz held to his ear, one after another, a series of globe-shaped resonators which responded to different frequencies, and noted which ones strongly reinforced the sound. Nowadays, by means of a microphone, sounds are converted into electric currents, which vary with time just as the sound pressure or velocity does. Thus electrical circuits, which behave in a way exactly analogous to acoustic resonators, can be used to select components of various frequencies and so to analyze the sound.

Acoustic resonators are extremely important in the production of sound. If we speak into the mouth of a milk bottle we can sense that certain of the frequencies present in the sound waves of our voice are emphasized by the resonance of the bottle. In the reed stops of an organ the complex sounds produced by the reed are modified by a resonant pipe attached to it, so that certain frequencies are emphasized and others suppressed. Pipes of peculiar shape, such as the coned gamba, can, for instance, give a voicelike quality to the organ sound. It is the distribution of higher resonances in the tube that gives other reed instruments their characteristic qualities of sound.

Resonators may be used in producing sounds in a more direct manner. When the bellows blow across the mouth of the organ pipe of Fig. 3.7, the air inside is set into vibration. The pipe speaks at its fundamental frequency (f_0 or f_1 of Fig. 3.7). Because the pipe is resonant at multiples of this frequency, these harmonic frequencies are excited by the puffs of air at the throat; so sounds of many related frequencies compose the note of the organ.

It is only in resonators of very simple form that the higher frequencies are harmonics of (that is, multiples of) the lowest or fundamental frequency. For instance, consider a pipe closed at the left end and with a sliding shutter at the right, as shown at the top of Fig. 3.9. If the shuttered end is completely open, the velocity patterns will be as shown in *a* below; the first resonant frequency will be f_0 and the

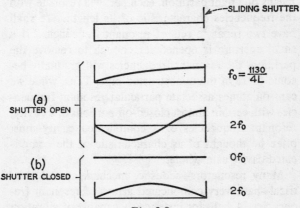

SLIDING SHUTTER

$$f_0 = \frac{1130}{4L}$$

$2f_0$

(a)
SHUTTER OPEN

$0f_0$

(b)
SHUTTER CLOSED

$2f_0$

Fig. 3.9

59

next higher will be $3f_0$; the ratio of the lowest two frequencies is 3. If we close the shutter completely, the velocity patterns will be as shown in b. The two lowest resonant frequencies will be *zero* and $2f_0$ and the ratio of these is a very large number—namely, infinity. If we start with the shutter open and close it gradually, the velocity patterns will pass smoothly from those of a to those of b. The two lowest resonant frequencies will both fall, and the ratio between them will gradually increase from 3 to very large values. In the intermediate range the resonant frequencies will not be harmonically related.

Closing the shutter at the right end of the pipe of Fig. 3.9 affects its resonant frequencies. Similarly, closing the lips affects the resonant frequencies of the human vocal tract, a matter which we shall consider in Chapter VII. There we shall also note that the human vocal tract can be divided into two distinct regions by the humping of the tongue.

Clearly, if we divide a long pipe into two parts by means of a tight partition, each part will resonate with the frequencies characteristic of its length. We shall have two separate sets of resonant frequencies. If a small aperture is opened far enough to remove the partition, the resonant frequencies will gradually become those of the unobstructed pipe. Thus, while we can sometimes associate particular resonant frequencies with certain almost closed-off portions of a cavity, resonant frequencies of a complicated cavity must often be thought of as characteristic of the complicated cavity as a whole.

Many resonators—acoustic, mechanical and electrical—have very complicated arrays of resonant frequencies. A bell, for instance, is capable of vibration at an irregular series of frequencies. When the clapper strikes it, these vibrations are all set up at once, and a clangorous sound of many non-harmonically related frequencies is produced. A stretched string, however, vibrates at frequencies that are multiples of the fundamental frequency, and to our ears the sound of plucked or bowed strings has a more "musical" quality than that of a struck bell.

Music and Noise

Musical instruments are essentially complex resonators. Depending on their geometrical shape, they emphasize certain harmonics in the complex sound that is put into them by the mouthpiece, strings, reeds, or other sources of *excitation*. This is visible in Fig. 3.10 (see Plates), which is a spectrogram of some common instruments. A spectrogram is a plot of frequency (on the vertical axis) against time (horizontal axis). The degree of blackness of the lines is a measure of the intensity. The musicians held a steady note (middle A), so there is very little variation in time. If you compare the picture of the sound of the trumpet mouthpiece with that of the sound of the complete trumpet, you can readily note the difference. The resonator (the trumpet horn, essentially a conical type) decreases the first harmonic (fundamental) slightly, emphasizes the second and third harmonics, transmits the fourth one pretty much unaltered, and all but rejects the fifth harmonic. There are many more appreciably higher harmonics, which do not show up in this picture. The curious "hash" in the higher frequencies of the mouthpiece (also visible in the violin spectrogram) is something approaching *gaussian noise,* which contains all frequencies equally and which we shall discuss shortly in some detail; here it is blowing and bowing noise. As you can see, the differences in the various wind instruments are mostly a matter of the relative strength of the harmonics.

Musical sounds are periodic; that is, they repeat periodically in time. Fig. 3.11 illustrates the variation

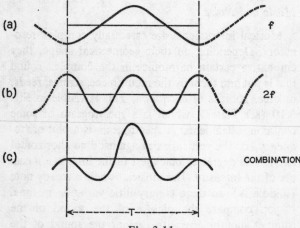

Fig. 3.11

of sound pressure with time for a particular periodic sound made up of two components having frequencies f and $2f$. In a we see how the pressure of the component of frequency f varies with time: it returns to its original value in a time, $T = 1f$. In b we see how the pressure of the component of frequency $2f$ varies with time: it returns to its original value in a time $\frac{1}{2}T$ and again in a time T, and so on. The sum of the pressures, shown in c, also returns to its original value in a time T. Any periodic sound that returns to its original value in a period T can be analyzed or broken up into component sinusoidal sounds of frequencies $1/T, 2/T, 3/T$, and so on. Our ears tell us that the pitch of a periodic sound is the frequency with which it repeats itself: $1/T$ in Fig. 3.11. This is true even if the periodic sound has no sinusoidal component of the pitch frequency.

We get a periodic sound if we momentarily excite a resonator (pluck a string, for instance) whose natural frequencies are all multiples of some fundamental frequency. In the simplest case we may excite only one resonant frequency. Such sounds are not quite truly periodic, however. The amplitude of the oscillation decays smoothly with time. Fig. 3.12 shows

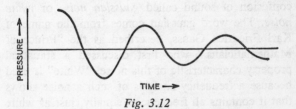

Fig. 3.12

this for the excitation of a single resonant frequency.

If several resonant frequencies are excited, the amplitudes may decay at different rates as the sound dies out, and so the shape of the wave may alter gradually with time during its decay. We notice this in piano sounds. A bass note of the piano alters somewhat in quality after it is struck, being initially more clangorous and becoming more mellow as it dies away.

When we excite at a single instant a resonator (a

bell, for instance) for which the higher frequencies are not multiples of the lowest frequency, we get a clangorous, noisy sound, although certain frequencies may be nearly enough in a harmonic relation to make the sound almost periodic, and to give us a sense of pitch.

When we hear many unrelated sounds together, we characterize the confused sum of them all as noise. While a noise can be analyzed into component frequencies, the multitudinous frequency components have little relation to one another.

At the end of the range of sound quality extending from pure sine waves through musical tones consisting of an assortment of harmonically related frequencies, on to clangorous sounds, and beyond the incomplete chaos of ordinary noises, there is a pure confusion of sound called *gaussian noise* or *white noise*. The word gaussian comes from the name of Karl Friedrich Gauss, described as the "Prince of Mathematicians," who first discussed a statistical property characteristic of this noise. "White" is used because a frequency analysis of such a noise shows that it contains all frequencies equally, just as white light is made up of all frequencies or colors of light. Gaussian noise is much like a hiss, a *shh* or a *sss*, though low frequencies tend to be absent in these sounds. An electrical signal corresponding to gaussian noise can be produced by means of gas tubes and other electronic gadgets. It is useful in acoustic experiments and devices.

Every moment of our lives we are surrounded by sounds, ranging from the hush of the night to the din of traffic, and embracing music and articulate speech. The power of the loudest of them is low by other standards, and the power of the fainter sounds we hear is almost unthinkably small; yet they and their components of various frequencies travel independently, without interaction.

Sounds and mixtures of sounds exhibit complex variations of pressure with time, but the complexity, however great, can be thought of as a mixture of sinusoidal sound waves of different frequencies and powers.

Nature, art, and science provide tools appropriate to this vast world of sound. Closed or almost-closed cavities (that is, resonators) respond strongly to sounds of certain frequencies. When we put a sea shell to our ear, we hear the "sound of the sea" because the resonances of the shell emphasize certain frequencies in the noise about us. We can use acoustic resonators or their electric analogues to analyze a complicated sound into component sounds of the different frequencies and wavelengths of which all sounds are made. We can use electric circuits to amplify and to measure sounds both faint and strong. We can use an electric device called an oscillograph to trace out the way the pressure of a sound varies with time—a curve such as those of Figs. 3.11 and 3.12.

We can also use resonators, and electronic devices as well, to produce sounds and to reinforce certain frequencies in periodic sounds. Here we have before us the whole wonderful field of music. Sounds are the raw material of human communication. Whatever is not arbitrary about language is determined in part by the structure of the organs used to produce human speech and in part by the capabilities and limitations of our sense of hearing. But language also is constrained and shaped by the acoustics, by the properties of frequency and velocity, and by the consequent phenomena of interference and resonance characteristic of sound. The very anatomy and physiology of speech and hearing must conform to the facts of acoustics. Thus an understanding of acoustics is necessary to an understanding of man and his sounds.

CHAPTER IV

What Do We Hear?

Some years ago a man I know who works at an industrial research laboratory noticed, as he drove through the New Jersey meadows in the evening, that the crickets all seemed to chirp in unison and with the same pitch. Could he, he wondered, make an electronic supercricket and influence the chirping of this vast horde of insects?

The idea so fascinated him that he sought the help of two colleagues. He himself made an electronic device which produced, as nearly as he could tell, authentic-sounding cricket chirps of variable pitch and of variable repetition rate. His colleagues constructed a powerful portable amplifier and speaker system. One summer evening they loaded all this electronic gear into a station wagon, took it to a suitable location along the highway, pulled off the road, and started to set up the equipment. A suspicious state trooper soon stopped to ask what they were doing. The three scientists explained. This was in the early days of the war, and the trooper was understandably suspicious. He told them to pack up and get going.

The three did not give up their project, however. By some means they succeeded in getting the gear set up in a favorable location at a favorable time. They twiddled the dials, emitting giant cricket chirps at various rates and pitches, but in vain. The crickets went happily on at their own rate and pitch, paying no attention to electronic chirps, large or small.

Baffled, the three scientists loaded up their apparatus and went home. The chief investigator then sought out the name of a world authority on crickets and wrote the whole sad story to this English cricket expert. The expert politely informed him that while crickets do emit a sound audible to human ears, there is also an ultrasonic component to the stridulation (the crickets' grating noise), a sound too high in pitch for our hearing. It is only this latter ultrasonic vibration that the crickets themselves hear. The experimenters had produced a tremendous noise to which the crickets were entirely deaf!

Riddles of Hearing

The moral of this story would appear to be that we hear only what we can hear, and that there may be a great many obvious differences among sounds which must forever escape our ears. We should note that a person who speaks a language with an accent may not hear the difference between his speech and that of those who pronounce the words properly. This is a real defect in his sense or use of hearing, to be sure, but it is one attributable to his lack of training—as are the clumsy movements of an unskilled dancer—not to a defect in him as human raw material. There are, however, limits beyond which the human ear cannot be trained to make distinctions, although these vary somewhat from person to person. As we shall see, some sounds are too faint to be heard even when we know that they are present. Some changes in intensity or pitch can be below the threshold of detectability. A loud sound may mask a weak one, although with electrical apparatus we could easily detect the presence of the weak sound. Something of the limitations of our sense of hearing will be discussed in this chapter.

First, however, it is important to make another point about human hearing. To some degree we hear what we expect to hear. Recently an expert in psychoacoustics familiarized a group of subjects with a certain piece of choral music by playing it to them repeatedly until they knew it very well. He then played the music to each of the subjects in the presence of a loud white noise and gradually lowered the volume of the music to zero. He asked each subject to indicate at what point the music disappeared. The subjects all heard the music for a considerable time after it had been turned off.

Had the subjects fabricated the music they heard out of nothing, or had they in some way shaped it out of the chaotic pattern of noise reaching their ears? It is hard to tell. Similar phenomena are, however, fairly common in everyday experience. The first time I tried to go somewhere on the Long Island Railroad I interpreted the garbled sound emitted by the conductor at a stop as the name of my destination and got off ten miles too soon. After the birth of his first child a friend of mine became very sensitive to the sound of a baby's crying. He would continually rush to see what the trouble was, only to find his son peacefully asleep. He had heard in the sound of a washing machine, or in some other unrelated noise, the crying he was listening for.

It is cheap and easy to listen to a sound—to a voice, to a record—and then to sit back and meditate, philosophize, and draw conclusions about what one has heard. This may be useful at times, but it is very fallible. People can learn to tolerate or even to like distorted sound. I know a fellow who speaks with a strong accent. People have repeatedly told me after knowing him for a few months that his speech has improved. It hasn't; they have adapted themselves to his accent. A similar confusion is to be noted in those who have built artificial speaking machines of one sort or another. Their machines always sound amazingly intelligible and natural to them, however peculiar they may sound to others. I am sure, too, that it is just as easy to sense unreal distinctions as it is not to hear real ones.

Thus psychologists and psychoacousticians handle subjective data (that is, data in which we have only the subject's word concerning an effect) very gingerly. To a degree people hear—and people see, for that matter—what they expect to hear and see. We should not deplore this, but we should accept it as a fact of life and be ever conscious of it in our experiments. With a wary mind and a sense of human limitation, then, let us find out as nearly as we can what we do hear.

In Chapter II we saw that the sounds audible to the human ear cover a range of sound power of around a million million times, or 120 db. Sounds of all frequencies can be felt as a tickling of the ears at about the same intensity of 120 db above reference level, but the least sound we can hear varies a great deal with frequency. Our hearing is most acute at a frequency of around 3000 cycles per second, which is between three and four octaves above middle C.

The United States Public Health Service has made a survey of the hearing acuity of a typical group of Americans. The results are shown in Fig. 4.1. Here

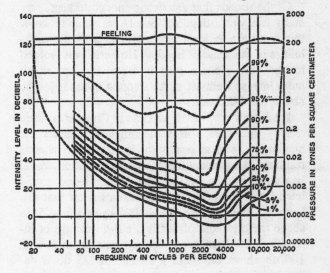

Fig. 4.1

we have the least sound which can be heard, in decibels above reference level plotted against frequency. There are curves labeled 1 per cent, 5 per cent, 10 per cent, etc. Consider the 10 per cent curve, for instance. The meaning of this curve is that 10 per cent of the group could hear a sound as weak as, or weaker than, the curve indicates. It is generally considered that the 1 per cent curve represents "normal" hearing

71

(for a healthy young adult), while the other curves represent "impaired hearing." It is clear, however, that by this standard most people have impaired hearing.

The Ear's Powers of Discrimination

Of the sounds that are strong enough to hear, how many can we distinguish? Surely we want to know this if we are to form any useful idea of the capabilities of our sense of hearing. How shall we proceed to find out? We can start by observing how much more intense we must make a sound in order just to notice the difference.

If Weber's law, which we cited in Chapter II, were exactly true, then, within the range of intensity the human ear hears as sound, the least intensity change resulting in a perceptible change in sensation would be a constant number of decibels, regardless of sound intensity or frequency. Measurements show that this is not so. For instance, for a 1000-cycle sound 5 db above the threshold of hearing, a 3-db change of intensity is the least detectable by ear, but at a level 100 db above threshold a change of .25 db is detectable. For a 35-cycle sound 5 db above threshold, the minimum perceptible change is over 9 db. Were we perhaps wrong in valuing Weber's law so highly?

Suppose that we had reckoned sound intensity directly in terms of watts per square centimeter. We find that the minimum perceptible difference in power at 1000 cycles is about .0000003 billionth watt per square centimeter for a sound intensity 5 db above threshold, but it is 60 billionths of a watt per square centimeter at an intensity 100 db above threshold.

These two powers differ in a ratio of two hundred million, while the corresponding minimum detectable differences in intensity of 3 db and .25 db differ in ratio by only 12. If Weber's law is inexact, it is still a good general guide in thinking about our sense of hearing. Certainly we did well to measure sound intensity in accord with it.

We must be concerned with differences in frequency or pitch as well as with differences in sound intensity. Careful measurements have been made of the minimum detectable change in pitch for pure sinusoidal tones of various frequencies and intensities. In sounds of moderate level, one can detect a change of pitch of about 3 cycles per second for frequencies below 1000 cycles per second (two octaves above middle C). For higher frequencies the minimum detectable difference is a constant fraction of the frequency, amounting to about one semitone.

By considering the minimum detectable change in sound intensity as compared with the total intensity range of audible sound, we would conclude that there are some 280 discriminably different intensity levels of sound. Data on minimum detectable pitch difference indicate that there are some 1400 discriminably different pitches of sound. We might naively multiply these numbers and assert that the human ear can discriminate among some 400,000 simple, single-frequency sounds differing in pitch and amplitude only. If we added to this the larger group of complex sounds consisting of many frequencies, with what powers of discrimination might we credit the human ear?

All this is very misleading, for the experiments producing the numbers are far removed from our common experience. We can see this by considering a similar case. Suppose you were supplied with half a million photographs of different faces. It is easy to believe that if you compared them carefully you could distinguish any two. This does not mean, however, that you could learn to recognize or distinguish among half a million faces, viewing each one at a separate time.

The human ear perhaps can discriminate among some 400,000 similar sounds in the sense of telling that there is a difference between any two when the two are presented in rapid succession under favorable conditions. We can think of a different and more realistic experiment, however, an experiment which has been carried out by a skeptical psychologist named Irwin Pollack. Suppose an average person is allowed to hear separately but repeatedly a number of tones differing in frequency and intensity and asked to remember each in terms of pitch and loudness. He then hears one sound and is asked which sound among the familiar group it is. The astonishing result of some experiments is that people seem unable to classify sounds beyond about seven degrees of loudness and seven degrees of pitch. In this experiment people were able to distinguish among about seven times seven or forty-nine tones of different pitch and loudness, hearing them one at a time. It is interesting to note that this is not far from the number of *phonemes* we distinguish in a language. (A phoneme is the smallest unit in a language that distinguishes one utterance from another; we discuss them further in Chapter VII.) Certainly it is nearer to the number of phonemes than is the number of 400,000 sounds which we might carelessly have inferred from measurements of the just discriminable changes in loudness and pitch.

We may be reminded that people with absolute pitch can discriminate unerringly among far more than seven frequencies heard one at a time, but then, how fast can they do it? Whatever we are to believe concerning the number of distinguishable sounds, we must be careful to think of what we mean by the term, and we must be sure that the data on which we base our estimates are pertinent to what we have in mind.

So far we have talked about the sounds to which human beings are exposed in terms of intensity, or power, which we can measure with electronic equipment, and of frequency, which we can measure with other equipment. Intensity and frequency are valuable because we can pin them down and show what they mean.

Measuring Loudness and Pitch

In measuring our human ability to hear faint sounds and to detect differences in intensity and frequency we are approaching that inner world of sound —the world of the sound of a voice or the song of a lark, the world in which we make a distinction between a click and a thunderclap. How far can we go into this world of the sensation of sound by means of experiment rather than philosophy or rhapsody?

A simple starting point in such a quest is to ask, can we consistently relate the different loudness of tones of different frequencies? In investigating this we can present to people alternately two tones of different frequencies and different intensities and ask them to judge which is the louder. When the intensities of two tones of different frequencies are such that on the average a subject is equally likely to judge either tone to be the louder, the two tones can be said to be equally loud. Gratifyingly, it turns out that if two different tones are equal in loudness to a third tone, they are themselves equally loud when compared directly to one another.

Perhaps you do not see immediately what there is to be grateful about; after all, if $a = b$ and $b = c,$ then $a = c$. Such simple logical rules, however, do not always hold for psychological measurements and quantities, especially not when the stimuli are different in other aspects in addition to the one we try to measure. For instance, I recently tried an experiment in which I compared the speech transmission systems A, B and C, each with its own peculiar-sounding but easily recognizable distortion. I compared them two at a time: A to B, B to C, and A to C, and added increasingly intense white noise until my listeners could not tell them apart any longer. The noise level at that point gives me a sort of measure of the *difference* between the two systems at hand. It turned out, much to my distress, that the difference between A and B was greater than the difference between A and C, but that the difference between C and B was greater than the difference of A and B! Fortunately, in comparing loudness of single tones we do not run into this sort of complication.

It is possible to specify the different frequencies and intensities of tones that seem equally loud in the subject's judgment. This has been done in Fig. 4.2, whose curves relate human sensations of loudness to intensities and frequencies of sound. Let us consider, for example, the curve labeled 60. To the subject's

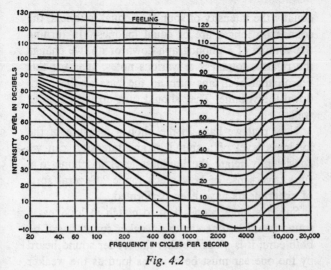

Fig. 4.2

ear a sound at any point on this curve seems as loud as a sound at any other point although the frequencies and intensities of the two will be different. Thus, if you follow the curve from the 1000-cycle tone with an intensity level of 60 db, you will see that a 100-cycle tone must have an intensity level of 72 db to be equally loud, and a 6000-cycle tone needs an intensity level of 68 db. Any such sound has a *loudness level* of 60 *phons*. The loudness level in phons of any tone is the intensity in decibels above reference level of a 1000-cycle tone of equal loudness.

We see from Fig. 4.2 that among loud sounds equal intensities give about equal loudnesses, regardless of frequency. At very low levels loudness is more nearly governed by the sound level in decibels above threshold. In an intermediate range the relation between intensity and loudness is intermediate. If we increase

77

equally the intensity of sounds of equal loudness, the sounds no longer are of equal loudness. In turning the volume of a phonograph down or up, we change the relative loudness of various notes. It is for this reason that hi-fi fans turn up the bass as they turn down the volume. They should turn up the treble as well.

Now that we have in the phon a measure of the loudness level of a sound of any intensity, can we consistently relate the loudness level in phons to a subjective sense of how much louder? Several sorts of experiments have been performed.

Subjects have been asked to match in loudness a sound heard by one ear to a weaker sound heard by both ears; it is plausible that the louder sound heard by the one ear must be twice as loud as the weaker sound heard by both ears if the listener is to have a subjective sense of the same loudness.

Experimenters also have asked subjects to match a sound in loudness to the sum of two other sounds of well-separated frequencies but of equal loudness; again it is plausible that the sound equaling the two in loudness must be twice as loud as either of them.

In other tests the subjects have been asked simply to judge when one sound is twice or half as loud as another, or when a sound is halfway between two others in loudness.

The results of experiments of this sort agree in general although doubling and halving may give somewhat different results. Some experiments, too, give more reproducible results than others. Because a comparison of the loudness of two tones with that of one tone gives very reproducible results, and results which agree with other methods, the loudness curve of Fig. 4.3 was obtained by this means.

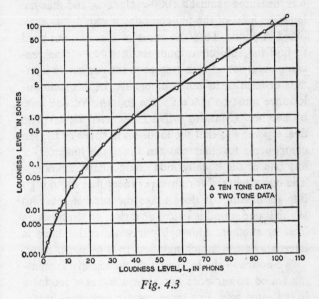

Fig. 4.3

Here the *subjective loudness* in *sones* is plotted against the loudness level in phons. Arbitrarily, 40 phons are taken to be 1 sone. A sound of 2 sones loudness is, for instance, twice as loud as a sound of 1 sone; to double the subjective loudness requires that we increase the loudness level in phons by about 9 db. This 9-db rule holds for more intense sounds, but for weak sounds subjective loudness in sones increases more rapidly with loudness level in phons.

The curve of Fig. 4.3 has been tested experimentally for sounds having ten components of different frequencies, each separately of the same loudness

level in phons (as compared with a 1000-cycle tone).
The loudness in phons of all ten components together
was measured against a 1000-cycle tone, and thus the
loudness level of the ten-component sound was eval-
uated in phons. Then the curve of Fig. 4.3 was used
to find the subjective loudness in sones of the ten-
component sound with respect to the subjective loudness of each of its ten components. In this some al-
lowance must be made for the *masking* of one tone
by another. (Masking will be discussed later.) The
final answer was that the loudness in sones of the ten
components together was ten times the loudness of
any one of the equally loud components separately.
The curve worked for an experiment that did not go
into its making! It does make measurable sense to
say that one sound is twice, or thrice, or ten times as
loud as another. Although our sense of loudness is
internal, we can attach numbers to it by experiment.

We notice in the foregoing discussion that increasing sound power does not always increase loudness
in the same way. For tones not far separated in frequency, equal powers give almost equal loudnesses.
Thus, when we double the power of a sound by adding to it a tone of equal power that differs not greatly
but sufficiently in frequency, we approximately double
the loudness. But if we double the power of a single
tone, we do not nearly double its loudness. In fact,
except for faint sounds, we must increase the intensity of a tone by 9 db, thus increasing its power
eight times, in order to double its loudness. However,
we see from Fig. 4.3 that doubling the power of a
very faint sound more than doubles its loudness. So
for such faint sounds a single sound is louder than

two sounds having different frequencies but the same total power.

If we simultaneously sound two tones not sufficiently separated in frequency, the two tones will not be twice as loud as each singly. Clearly we are in each case dealing with some sort of critical frequency range, or *bandwidth*. If two tones are separated by more than this bandwidth, the loudness of one adds to the loudness of the other; if they are not, the simple addition does not occur. At large intensity levels (70 db and above) this bandwidth becomes broader, and the loudness does not add even when the tones are considerably separated in frequency.

Besides a scale of subjective loudness, acousticians have constructed a subjective scale for the pitch of pure tone or sine waves. Here the problem is different from that of loudness. You can imagine the loudness of two sounds adding, but it is ridiculous to think of their pitches adding. Thus the experiments involving *monaural* against *binaural* hearing, or those comparing two tones against one tone, which were used in establishing a scale of subjective loudness, are of no use in establishing a scale of pitch. Instead we must rely entirely on the subject's judgment whether the pitch of one tone is half as great or twice as great as that of another; whether the pitch of a tone lies midway between the pitches of two other tones; or whether the two intervals between two pairs of tones are equal.

The pitch scale constructed through such experiments is shown by the solid line of Fig. 4.4. Frequency is plotted horizontally, and pitch, measured in subjective units called *mels,* is plotted vertically. Two tones separated by a constant number of mels appear

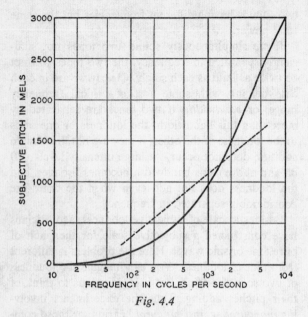

Fig. 4.4

equally far apart in pitch regardless of frequency. A tone whose pitch is twice as many mels as a second tone seems to have twice as high a pitch.

The dotted line in Fig. 4.4 is the curve we would get if a semitone or an octave represented an equal difference in pitch regardless of frequency. The experimental subjective pitch scale for pure tones is not at all like this. We can only conclude that for sine waves, at least, "equal" musical intervals do not represent equal intervals of subjective pitch.

This baffled me to the extent that I nearly left the mel scale out of this book. It does, however, represent real psychoacoustic data. Moreover, it is related to other important psychoacoustic data. The *limen,* or just noticeable difference in pitch, is a nearly constant number of mels—about $\frac{1}{20}$. The critical bandwidth within which the loudness of tones fails to add is about one mel. Another critical bandwidth (derived from masking experiments, which we will discuss in a moment) is a nearly constant number of mels wide, regardless of frequency. Moreover, frequency ranges which contribute equally to the intelligibility of speech are very nearly a constant number of mels wide. It would be odd if the agreement among these data were accidental.

I am now inclined to believe that the mel scale reflects a "place" mechanism in the ear, which will be discussed in Chapter V, while the scale of musical pitch is associated with a time-comparison phenomenon, which will be discussed in Chapter VI.

Interaction of Tones

Many of the most striking phenomena of hearing have to do with the interaction of tones or sounds heard simultaneously. Most of the experiments we have discussed so far have involved very special sounds seldom if ever found in nature—that is, sine waves or sounds of a single frequency. The nearest thing we ordinarily encounter is a whistle or the sound of a flute, but in listening to these musical tones we are usually more concerned with successions of notes of different but easily distinguished pitch and loudness than with a sustained tone itself.

Usually, and in speech especially, we are concerned with complicated sounds which we may think of as made up of many sinusoidal components having different frequencies. When such sounds travel through the air, we can treat each separate component of a particular frequency separately, for sound waves travel without interacting or changing one another in any way. What about our inner world of sound, our subjective experience of hearing?

There is a "law" of acoustics called Ohm's acoustical law. It states that when we are exposed to two tones simultaneously we have the distinct sensations characteristic of hearing each tone separately. This might seem merely to be extending the linear, noninteracting behavior of sound waves to the realm of sensation, but Ohm's law is really more drastic than this.

Ohm's acoustical law does refer to a true aspect of our hearing. Those of us who can identify the notes of a piano sounded one at a time can identify two notes on a piano, even when they are sounded simultaneously. The British acoustician Sir Richard Paget taught himself to hear the two lower resonances or *formants* of a whispered vowel. But the qualifications concerning Ohm's law, and the exceptions to it, are certainly as important as the law itself. For instance, we have seen that the loudness of one tone does not simply add to another unless the frequencies of the tones differ by more than some critical bandwidth. Thus the behavior of tones close together in frequency is contrary to Ohm's law in at least one way.

In order to understand something about the limitations of Ohm's law, we must appreciate that sinusoidal sound waves can differ in another respect than in intensity or frequency. Fig. 4.5 shows pressure plotted against time for five sinusoidal sound waves of the same frequency and amplitude. These waves differ in the time at which the air pressure is a maximum—at

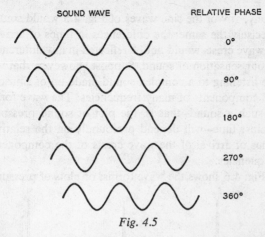

Fig. 4.5

the ear, for instance. Or we can say that they differ in the time at which the wave crest arrives at the ear.

It is perhaps worth mentioning that such a difference of time of arrival is called a difference of *phase*. If we let a component frequency arrive a half wavelength or a half period later, the change in phase is 180°; a whole period or a whole wavelength delay corresponds to a phase change of 360°, which has the same effect as no change at all. In Fig. 4.5 the phase of each sinusoidal wave is indicated at the right of the figure.

Now we may sense a certain throbbing in the sound of a very, very low note of a pipe organ, and so sense to a degree the times of arrival of the wave crests. For most audible frequencies, however, although we may have some sense of the sound's being vibratory in nature, we cannot sense at all the time of arrival of wave crests, and the sound of a sine wave of a high frequency is a smooth sensation of tone. Heard separately, any of the sine waves of Fig. 4.5 would sound precisely the same; the differences in times of arrival of wave crests would not be reflected in any difference in our sensation of sound. Suppose, however, that we are listening to a complex sound made up of sinusoidal components of many frequencies. The wave form of such a sound—that is, the plot of sound pressure against time—will depend profoundly on the relative times of arrival of the wave crests of the component frequencies.

Fig. 4.6 shows the wave forms, or plots of pressure

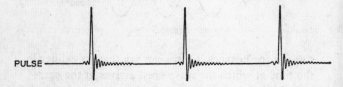

PULSE

Fig. 4.6

against time, for two such complex sound waves. Each wave is made up of thirty-two component sine waves of different frequencies. The wave forms of the two sounds differ because in the two sounds the crests of the component sine waves have different relative phases—that is, they arrive at different times relative to one another. While the relative phases of the components are different in the two waves, the frequencies and intensities of the components are the same for each.

Do the two sound waves of Fig. 4.6 sound the same to us? If Ohm's law were literally true, each component frequency of the sound would arouse in us a particular sensation, the same whether or not the other component frequencies were present. The sensations aroused by the different frequencies would be separate within us. As time of arrival does not affect the sensation when a single frequency is heard, it could not affect the sensation when many frequencies are heard, and the two sound waves of Fig. 4.6 should sound the same.

As a matter of fact, the two sound waves of Fig. 4.6 sound very different. The difference is perhaps best described by saying that the upper one sounds harsher and lower-pitched and somewhat louder than the lower one.

The ear is often said to be insensitive to phase. It is less sensitive to phase than are some electrical measuring instruments. Electric communication circuits often alter by a measurable amount the relative phases of sine waves of different frequencies passing over them, but usually this phase distortion is not great enough to alter the subjective quality of the speech transmitted over the circuit. Nevertheless, sufficiently great changes or differences in phase can and do alter the quality of a sound, as we have seen in connection with the sound waves of Fig. 4.6.

How Sounds Are Masked in the Ear

We have come upon failures in Ohm's law of acoustics in relation to loudness and quality of complex sounds, and we may expect others. Let us consider, for instance, complex sounds made up of com-

87

ponents of different intensities. We have seen that acoustic disturbances differing in power or intensity by 120 db can be heard as sound. If Ohm's law were strictly true, we should be able to detect a weak sound of one frequency in the presence of a sound of another frequency if the second sound was over 100 db more intense. This is perhaps too much to expect. It seems perfectly natural to us that loud sounds should tend to drown out weak sounds. Any electrical circuit devised to detect or sort our sounds would behave in a similar manner. The detailed way in which certain sounds drown out or *mask* others can, however, tell us a good deal about human hearing.

In listening to two sounds close together in pitch, we are strongly aware of the phenomenon of *beats,* a phenomenon scarcely in accord with Ohm's law. When we listen simultaneously to two sounds of comparable magnitudes but of slightly differing frequencies, the combined sound appears to us as a fluctuating sound of a single frequency. The frequency with which the amplitude fluctuates is the difference between the frequencies of the two beating sounds. The reason for this is easy to see. Fig. 4.7 shows in a and b two sound waves of slightly different frequencies, f_1 and f_2. The sum of these waves is shown in $a + b$. This sum wave looks very much like a wave of frequency f_2 whose amplitude varies with time.

In the case of very faint sounds this beating phenomenon completely disappears when the sounds are separated by some tens of cycles in frequency. In loud sounds, however, we hear the beat as a separate fainter sound of the difference frequency when this frequency lies in the range of audibility. This phenomenon must be associated with some sort of non-

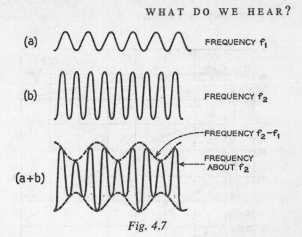

(a) — FREQUENCY f_1

(b) — FREQUENCY f_2

FREQUENCY $f_2 - f_1$

FREQUENCY ABOUT f_2

(a+b)

Fig. 4.7

linear response in the hearing mechanism. Sound waves traveling as linear waves through air do not distort one another. But somehow, between the excitation of the ear by sound and the sensation of sound in the brain, there is a non-linear phenomenon such that two strong sounds of different frequencies produce a third sound whose frequency is the difference between the frequencies producing it.

An understanding of the phenomenon of beats is necessary to understand fully the results of the elaborate masking studies which have been made to show in what degree a sound masks or hides a sound of some other frequency. The curves of Fig. 4.8 show the masking effect of sounds having frequencies of 400 cycles per second and 1200 cycles per second.

These curves tell us how intense a tone of a particular frequency has to be if we are just to hear it in the presence of the masking tone. Frequency is measured from left to right, and is identified in the bottom scale. The intensity in decibels above threshold (in the

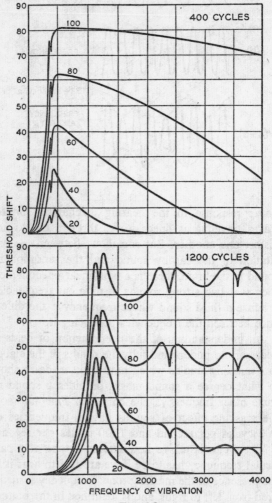

Fig. 4.8

absence of the masking tone) which a sound must have in order to be just heard in the presence of the masking tone is measured upward. In effect the masking tone raises the threshold of hearing by an amount dependent on frequency, and hence the vertical scale is labeled threshold shift.

The numbers 20, 40, 60, 80, 100 next to the masking curves indicate the intensity of the masking tone in decibels above threshold.

As an example, in the presence of a 400-cycle tone of intensity 80 db above threshold, how intense must a 2000-cycle tone be if we are just to hear it? The appropriate curve in the upper part of Fig. 4.8 tells us that, in order to be heard in these circumstances, the 2000-cycle tone must be 50 db above what would be the threshold of hearing if the masking tone were absent. In a sense, the 400-cycle tone has deafened us for 2000-cycle tones to this degree; it has certainly raised our threshold of hearing for 2000-cycle tones by 50 db.

We see by examining the masking curve of Fig. 4.8 that tones near in frequency to the masking tone are strongly masked. At high levels such tones are not heard at all if their intensity is 20 db or more below the intensity of the masking tone. At low levels the masking is even greater. When, however, the frequency of the masked tone nearly coincides with the frequency of the masking tone, the masking is somewhat less. This is because the presence of the masked tone is first evident not as a separate sound but, through the phenomenon of beats, as a fluctuation in the amplitude of the loud masking tone.

Let us consider particularly the masking curves for low sound intensities. As we have noted, tones far removed in frequency from a particular tone have little masking effect on that tone. What about masking by a noise that has sinusoidal components of many frequencies? We surmise that only those components whose frequencies are fairly near a given tone will tend to mask it. Thus we can define a critical bandwidth for masking. Only the part of the noise power associated with frequencies lying in this bandwidth around the tone has a masking effect on the tone. This critical bandwidth, therefore, expresses the range of frequency over which the sensations caused by two sounds are not experienced independently but are affected by one another. It is when the frequencies of several tones lie within a similar critical bandwidth that the loudness of their sum is not the sum of the separate loudnesses. But the critical bandwidths for noise masking and for loudness summation are not the same. The latter is about 2.5 times larger than the former.

These critical bandwidths increase with frequency. We recall that the least discriminable change in frequency also increases with frequency. As was mentioned, for a given frequency above 100 cycles per second the critical bandwidth for masking is almost exactly twenty times the least change in frequency that can be noticed at the given frequency. This implies a relationship between the fineness of frequency discrimination and the masking of one tone by others. A similar statement can be made about frequency discrimination and loudness summation. Further, the contribution of various bands of frequencies to the intelligibility of speech appears to vary in the same way with frequency. It could be that some basic physiological fact underlies these relations.

Let us return to masking, and consider a feature particularly noticeable at high sound levels. We notice in the curves for masking by a 1200-cycle sound (Fig. 4.8) that if the masking sound is loud, a similar phenomenon occurs at harmonics of the masking frequency (2400 cycles; 3600 cycles). A loud tone produces beats with other tones having its harmonic frequencies as well as with other tones of the same frequency. This is a manifestation of a non-linear characteristic of the hearing mechanism, and it is important at high sound levels.

If we examined the curves of Fig. 4.8 too casually, we might conclude that a sound of a certain frequency masks sounds of higher frequencies much more than it masks sounds of lower frequencies. This is true only for sounds of high intensity. Indeed, at a low intensity, a sound of frequency f_1 may mask a sound of frequency f_2 more than it masks a sound frequency f_3, while at a higher intensity a sound of frequency f_1 may mask a sound of frequency f_3 more than a sound of frequency f_2.

Harvey Fletcher, an early investigator of psychoacoustics, gives an example of this. In listening to a complex sound containing frequencies of 400, 300, and 2000 cycles with levels of 50, 10, and 10 db, respectively, the loudest sound would so mask the 300-cycle sound that the ear would hear only the 400-cycle and the 2000-cycle components. If, however, the levels of all sounds were raised by 30 db, to 80, 40, and 40 db, respectively, then only the 400-cycle and the 300-cycle components would be heard. Thus the quality of this sound would change markedly with distance or loudness. Hi-fi enthusiasts are correct in maintaining that sound quality can be reproduced accurately only if the original loudness is re-created.

Von Békésy did a very interesting experiment in which he compared the vibration sensitivity of the skin, say of the forearm, with the sense of hearing. He constructed an array of vibrators as shown in Fig. 4.9, on which he had an observer lay his arm.

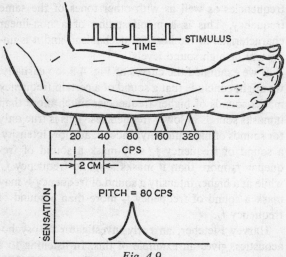

Fig. 4.9

Then he started all the vibrators at once at the same amplitude but at different frequencies, as shown in the drawing. The observer not only reported that the sensation seemed to be strongest in the center of the array, but he judged the pitch of this mixture of frequencies to be that of the vibrator in the center! The frequencies of the other vibrators were *masked*, but their vibration added to the "loudness" of the center sensation. Apparently the nervous impulses corresponding to the outside vibrators were inhibited, and somehow channeled into the "center" nerves; von Békésy calls this the "funneling" action of the nervous system.

Masking is extremely important in considering what we hear. Because of masking, we will be completely unaware of some of the fainter frequency components of a complex sound. Such components could be altered or eliminated without changing what we hear at all. Thus masking is one phenomenon that greatly reduces the number of sounds—of speech or of music—that *sound* different without exhibiting measurable physical differences.

Masking, as we have seen, concerns the rise of threshold for one tone in the presence of a second or masking tone. It has been shown that this shift does not disappear immediately when the masking tone is removed. Rather, the threshold falls relatively slowly to its resting value. We might describe this effect as a temporary hearing loss, and its value is known as auditory fatigue. The masking tone is usually called the fatiguing tone. The duration and severity of the fatigue depend upon the duration of the stimulation and its level. The longer and louder the stimulation, the greater are its effects. The fatigue is most prominent at frequencies above that of the fatiguing tone. For instance, immediately after exposure to a 110-db, 1000-cps tone for seven minutes, the 2000-cps thresholds of three subjects were raised an average of 45 db. After twenty-four hours there was still a 15-db fatigue. For softer and shorter sounds, the fatigue is much less severe. An effect of this kind is probably at the root of the common saying, "That sound was so loud that it deafened me."

A related phenomenon is that of auditory adaptation. This term refers to the fact that a sound is loudest when it first reaches our ears. Afterward the hearing sense adapts, and the subjective loudness decreases as time passes even though the intensity of the sound remains fixed.

Binaural Masking

There have been experiments to study the masking effect of a sound in one ear by a sound in the other ear. Here we find that a sound in one ear must be about 50 db more intense than the sound in the other ear before any masking effect is found. For louder sounds the masking is most plausibly explained if we assume that the masking sound reaches the opposite ear by shaking the bones of the head and does its masking there! It appears that we are able to listen independently with either ear—to connect either to the mind, so to speak.

When we listen with both ears, we are able to tell what direction a sound is coming from. It is clear that in some way we have the ability to compare and to combine the sounds as heard by the two ears, so as to get more information than we could obtain through either ear alone.

How do we compare the sounds reaching the two ears? Experiments make it clear that the relative amplitudes of the sounds reaching the two ears play an important part. This is particularly true for sounds made up of high frequencies, such as the sound of a small bell or chime. When the sounds have high frequency and short wavelength, the head casts an appreciable shadow so that the sound is considerably stronger in the ear turned toward the source than in the ear turned away from the source.

Experiments also show that relative time of arrival of the sound at the two ears plays an important part. This can be shown by performing an experiment in which sound from the same source is led to each ear independently. By the use of suitable electric networks the sound can be made to reach the right ear a few milliseconds (thousandths of a second) before or after it reaches the left ear, and the sound reaching the right ear can be made more or less intense than the sound reaching the left ear.

Now suppose we make the sound reach the right ear a millisecond or two later than it reaches the left ear. We find that if the sounds to the two ears are equally intense the sound seems to come from the left ear only. But, if we increase the intensity of the sound in the right ear enough, the sound will appear to be centered in the head, and not to come from either ear. By carrying out such an experiment we can get the data for a curve like that of Fig. 4.10. Here distance to the right depicts how much later the sound reaches the right ear than it reaches the left ear (negative numbers mean that it reaches the right ear first), and distance vertically depicts how much more intense in decibels the sound to the right ear must be in order that the sound may appear to be centered.

For complex sounds such as clicks, the behavior pictured in Fig. 4.10 is typical of sounds composed of either high or low frequencies. The behavior in the case of sinusoidal sound waves—that is, sounds of a single frequency—is somewhat more complicated.

We can, if we wish, think of a sine wave as made up of a number of successive pulses of sound, each

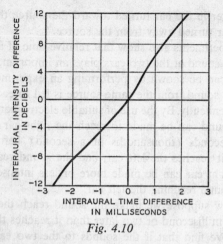

Fig. 4.10

contributing one peak or crest of the sine wave. Now, when pulses of sound reach the ear in too-rapid succession, the ear loses its power of time comparison. Thus differences of time of arrival between the two ears have no effect for pure tones (that is, sinusoidal sound waves) when the frequency of the sine wave is above perhaps 1500 cycles per second.

Time of arrival is important in the case of sinusoidal sound waves having frequencies below 1500 cycles per second. However, there is still a complication. A sine wave delayed one full period is the same as a sine wave not delayed at all. If we use a sine wave as a sound source, and if we make the sound arrive at the right ear increasingly later than at the left ear, the sound will first appear to move to the left side, then it will jump to the right side, then move to the left again, and so on.

Happily, speech sounds, music, and most natural sounds are not purely periodic, and they do not exhibit the complicated binaural effects we observe with the rather artificial sinusoidal sounds of the laboratory.

Our sense of direction can, however, behave in a very complicated way in listening to very ordinary sounds. In the 1930s, while they were working at the Bell Telephone Laboratories on stereophonic sound systems, two physicists, William B. Snow and John C. Steinberg, found that when the same sound reaches our ears from two sources at different distances, we hear the sound as coming from the nearer source rather than from both or from some intermediate point. Later observers found that when the times of arrival of the sounds from the two sources differ by a millisecond or more, this precedence effect—according to which we hear the sound as coming to us from the nearer source—persists until we make the source of delayed sound some 8 db more intense than the sound reaching the ears first. Our binaural sense of sound location works by comparing the sounds which come to the two ears. Perhaps the delayed sound gets there too late to be counted in the comparison!

Experience shows that noise and reverberation trouble us less when we are physically in a room with them than when we hear sounds sent to us from the room over a single channel by radio or TV. For this reason, radio and TV studios must have particularly good acoustics. When we are present in the flesh, we can concentrate our attention on the speaker by means of our binaural sense of direction. Also, the precedence effect helps us to ignore the echoes and reverberations. Although echoes and reverberations cause some frequencies in a complex sound to add at the ear and some to subtract, we usually do not notice a difference in sound quality except for very short or very long delays, for which the precedence effect is not strong.

Some Subtleties of the Ear

The precedence effect, startling as it is, is subjectively less odd than another effect involving binaural hearing. One day a colleague led me into a soundproof laboratory and asked me to stand at a particular point marked on the floor. Suddenly I heard a spooky voice say, "Members of the Second International Acoustics Conference: I am the Spirit of the Conference. You do not know where I am. I am reverberating inside that busy mind of yours. . . ."

Where was it? Not to the right, or to the left, or behind, or ahead, or up, or down. It was in the very center of my own head!

As illustrated in Fig. 4.11, my colleague had placed

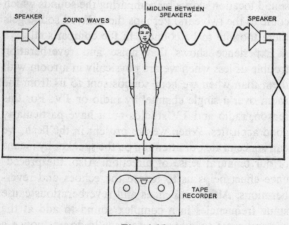

Fig. 4.11

speakers at equal distances from my two ears, and had fed one with a signal exactly the negative of the other; the same power and the same wave form, but upside down. My carefully trained sense of direction was completely confused and told me that the sound originated inside my skull. (This effect can be demonstrated only in an anechoic chamber—or in the open. Reflections from walls interfere with it.)

There are other odd effects concerning the hearing of sound, both monaural and binaural, but they are perhaps most interesting in connection with a consideration of the mechanisms of hearing. Here we have considered the range of hearing, our keenness of discrimination of intensity and pitch, how a valid quantitative meaning can be given to the subjective sense of loudness, the masking of one sound by another, and the phenomenon of beats. But with all this the reader may still feel cheated. What *do* we hear?

Certainly we do not hear separated, isolated frequencies, even when we are able to. When we hear many related frequencies sounded together, as they are in a familiar pattern of sound, we hear a familiar sound symbol, not a collection of frequencies. It is only with the most persistent "un-training" that we can hear a vowel sound as a collection of tones. Just try this if you doubt it. Our ability to analyze by ear a sound made up of many frequencies is limited. It is humanly impossible to hear a very complicated sound as a collection of separate frequency components.

With training, however, we can fuse many ill-assorted components into a single sound pattern, as we all do with vowel sounds. Thus an organist with advanced taste will savor as a piquant timbre what to the uninitiated seems a collection of wrong notes going along with the melody.

Neither do we hear each set of frequencies that reaches our ears as a separate sound. We will see that this is so in the case of diphthongs and glides, in which the frequency pattern slides quickly from that of one vowel to that of another. We hear not the two vowels in succession, but a new, distinct sound.

We do not hear instantaneously. Somehow a complicated sound which is a sequence of spectral patterns succeeding one another "rings in our ears" for a moment after we have heard it. It is during this moment that we can best imitate an unfamiliar sound. Of course, the sound does not truly ring in our ears; it is presumably stored momentarily in the brain—just how is not clear.

Most of our memories of sounds are of a different sort. They are not transient; they are permanent. We have stored in our heads a host of sound patterns. It is after these that we pattern our speech, and it is with the aid of these that we identify the words that we hear.

That these are learned patterns is clear. An Indian from a certain language group may be unable to hear the differences in the English words *park:bark, gross:grows, sweet:Swede, fine:vine, pluck:plug.* Yet the same Indian, and all others who speak his language and who exhibit this same defect of discrimination, insist that an English speaker's "p's" in *peel* and *pool* are two distinct sounds, and so are the "k's" in *kin* and *skin,* and the two "l's" in *lily.*

Words of an unknown tongue flow into our ears in a largely undifferentiated stream, yet we hear words of our own language with distinctness. Our ability to discriminate in this way grows with learning, but experience shows that such learning is a slow process. It is for this reason that I cannot take seriously simpleminded experiments purporting to show how many pitches or levels of sound we can recognize. It seems that the answer must depend largely on learning over a long period of time.

The most interesting sounds to us are complex sounds and complex sequences of sounds, and it is about the hearing of such sounds that we know the least. We know that our ability to discriminate among such sounds depends on training, but we do not know in any quantitative way how far such training can be carried.

We know that we perceive as a whole certain successions of sounds. Thus the short word *we* is very nearly the short word *you* said backward, yet the two sound very different to us. But over what range of time this phenomenon extends we do not know. Similarly, a sound "rings in our ears" for a moment after we have heard it, but for how long we do not know.

When we look back on the wonderful work that has been done on discrimination of pitch and intensity, on loudness, on masking, and on binaural hearing, we are heartened. Surely we will understand more complicated matters as well. And what lies ahead looks even more interesting than that which has been accomplished.

CHAPTER V

Ears to Hear with

Up to this point we have talked freely and frequently about our ability to hear, or about the sound waves striking an animal's ear, assuming without further question that there is something about or inside those adornments of the head, called *ears,* which makes us *hear.* That is to say, there must be something there that picks up the sound waves from our environment, and translates the pressure waves into something our brain will understand. Allow me to leave this last statement unexplained until a later chapter; let me just state that the brain understands *nerve impulses* only. Somehow, then, the ear transforms sounds into nerve impulses. This is its function, and its only function: to serve as a one-way translator from the language of the outside world (pressure waves) to the language of the "inside world" of the brain (nerve impulses). The voice mechanism, of course, is a one-way translator in the opposite direction. The obvious question now is, how does the ear accomplish this feat? Like most obvious questions, it is a very poor one; we are asking too much at once. And you might as well have the answer: we don't know yet. We still have to find out

densest and hardest bone in the body, lies the *inner ear*.

Now, the inner ear is so complex that we should divert our attention for a moment to its embryological development. I can demonstrate this best by sketching the growth of a frog. Not only is the frog a relatively simple animal as compared with the human being, but it is easily available from the earliest stage of development (the fertilized egg) and, consequently, has been thoroughly studied.

When the frog embryo is very young, and still inside the little jelly-ball that encloses the egg, the first signs of the developing ear become visible. In Fig. 5.1 I have sketched a frog embryo at that stage, with labels indicating the important structures that can be seen. You can distinguish head and tail, back and belly, the places where the gills of the future tadpole and its mouth will be, an eye bulge, and, finally, a small ridge, which is called *lateral placode*. This is what we are interested in, because it is the beginning of a whole set of organs of which the hearing organ is one. In the lower vertebrates such as the frog, other amphibians, and the fishes, the placode develops not only into an ear, but also into the *lateral line organ*.

If you have ever examined a fish—trout, carp, catfish—you may have noticed the line or streak that runs along the side of the body in the manner illustrated in Fig. 5.2. That streak is the visible indication of a long-stretched organ that really lies beneath the skin. The lower half of Fig. 5.2 is a cross section, considerably enlarged, through the lateral line. The lateral line canal is a long tunnel in the skin, and on the bottom of this tunnel stand, at more or less regular intervals, clusters of *sensory cells,* which make contact

107

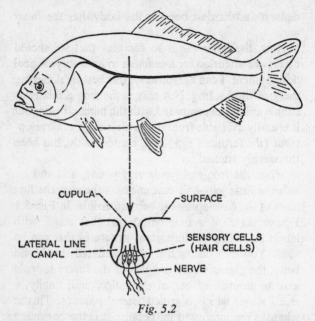

Fig. 5.2

with *nerve fibers*. The sensory cells have a very fine filament or hair at their tops; they are often called *hair cells*. The hair cells are the ultimate *transducers*, which translate motion into something the nerves "understand." The hairs are embedded in a gelatin-like *cupula*.

When prey, say a worm, moves through the water nearby, small alternating pressure differences are generated inside the lateral line canal; as the cupula is displaced by the minute water-currents that result from the pressure differences it bends, and tugs at the hairs, which somehow change something in the sensory cells, which then, somehow, excite the nerve. This seems to be a Rube Goldberg way of going about the business of telling the nervous system that there is a worm nearby, but, as you can see from the several "somehows" and "somethings" I have had to use, we really do not know precisely how it is done. It may turn out (as it almost always does) that Nature built the system very efficiently and that *we* could not do the job as effectively in another way unless it were to be even more complicated.

I have digressed quite far from my announced intent to trace the development of the frog's ear, and for the soundest of reasons. For, as we shall soon see, the whole complex structure of the inner ear can be thought of as having been built with the same units or building blocks that we find in the lateral line organ: clusters of hair cells with cupulae. Let us now return to the developing frog embryo. A day or so after our frog embryo reaches the stage of Fig. 5.1, there appears in the middle of the lateral placode a little dimple, which becomes deeper and deeper, until finally the skin around it closes up, thus forming under the skin a little bubble of placode tissue. This is called the *otic vesicle*. The vesicle continues to grow rapidly and soon looks like a small fluid-filled sphere. Then, quite suddenly, it starts taking on an hourglass shape by constricting in the middle, until it is almost —but not quite—pinched in two. Fig. 5.3 shows the various stages of this process as they would appear if you made thin sections through the frog's ear-region at the proper times. Although the two parts of the vesicle are still connected, they proceed to develop rather differently and for this reason are best treated separately. The upper, or *superior* part (*superior* and *inferior* in anatomical lingo mean just "upper" and "lower" and have no connotation of quality) develops

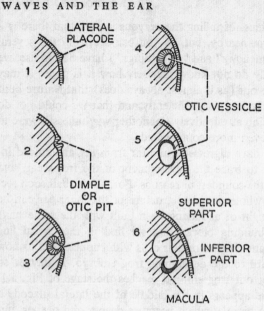

Fig. 5.3

into a set of organs sensitive to position with respect to gravity, and to rotation; these are usually called *equilibrium senses*. Although they are fascinating to study in their own right and present a whole set of ill-understood phenomena, it would lead us too far astray to describe them in detail. The lower, or *inferior,* part, on the other hand, develops into the structures used for sound perception, and that is after all our main interest here. The first sign that something is going to happen, as I have indicated in the last drawing of Fig. 5.3, is that the wall of the vesicle shows a thickening. When we examine this part with a microscope, we find that this thickening consists of cells of a rather different type from the rest of the vesicle; they are the special cell-type that develops into sensory, or hair, cells. They are, in fact, the same sort of cell that meanwhile has become visible also in the lateral line organ of our developing frog. Only here, inside the ear vesicle, the cells do not occur in small clusters, but in fairly large patches, called *maculae* (singular: *macula*). In such a young ear as that illustrated in Fig. 5.3, you would see only one macula, but as the frog grows this single sensory patch divides, and many (in the frog, four) definitive maculae of different sizes result. At the same time the original roundish vesicle becomes distorted by bulges, pinches, and protrusions, until at hatching time it looks something like Fig. 5.4. The bulges, of course, have names.

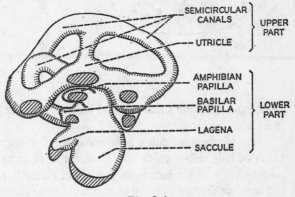

Fig. 5.4

The largest part—you might think of it as the original vesicle—is called the *saccule*. The protuberances are named *lagena, amphibian papilla* (it occurs only in amphibians), and *basilar papilla*. The maculae are called, logically: saccular macula, lagenar macula,

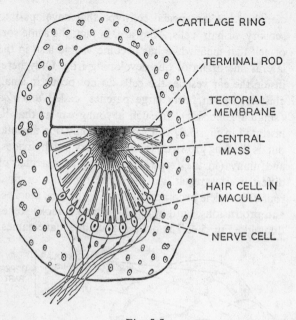

CARTILAGE RING

TERMINAL ROD

TECTORIAL MEMBRANE

CENTRAL MASS

HAIR CELL IN MACULA

NERVE CELL

Fig. 5.5a

amphibian (papillar) macula, and basilar (papillar) macula.

Each of these maculae now consists of a large patch of hair cells (which now have a tuft of hairs, rather than a single hair as in the lateral line cells), but here, unlike the lateral line organ, separate cupulae are no longer to be found. Instead, the maculae are covered with a jellylike mass, which in some cases (as in the saccular macula, for instance) accumulates crystals of a calcium compound, resulting in an *ear stone* or *otolith;* in other cases—for example, the two papillae—the jelly takes on the shape of a membrane.

Because these membranes cover up the macula, they are called *tectorial membranes* (from Latin: *tectum,* roof). Again the miscroscope is helpful in finding from where those membranes have arisen. It turns out that they are composed of individual cupulae (the same type as found in the lateral line) fused side by side into a single membrane. In Fig. 5.5a is illustrated the basilar papilla of a frog. Inside a stiff ring of cartilage lies the macula with its hair cells and nerves (I have drawn only one row; think of it as several layers deep). Edge-on atop the macula, somewhat like a curtain hanging down from the stiff *terminal rod,* is the *tectorial membrane,* with the hair tufts of the sensory cells embedded in it. As the photograph (of a different species of frog) shows very clearly (Fig. 5.5b, see Plates), the membrane consists of fused cupulae. The *central mass* is apparently a pile-up of surplus cupula material. For the physics of sound perception in the frog this central mass is very important, as we shall see later.

Structure of the Cochlea

Anatomists believe that the basilar papilla is the primitive hearing organ from which in the course of evolution the hearing organ of the mammals and man, the *cochlea,* developed. In reptiles and birds we find structures that can be thought of as being intermediate stages in this evolutionary process.

Let us now examine the anatomy of the cochlea. The word *cochlea* is Latin and means snail. It is a well-chosen word, because the cochlea actually looks like a snail shell (see Fig. 5.14). Fig. 5.6 is a sketch of a cochlea, unrolled to show its parts more clearly.

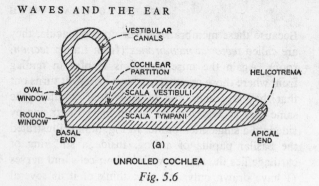

UNROLLED COCHLEA

Fig. 5.6

It is about 1⅓ inches long and perhaps ⅛ inch wide at its broadest point. Along most of its length it is divided by the *cochlear partition* into two sections, called the scala tympani and the scala vestibuli. These regions are filled with *perilymph fluid*. The scala tympani is separated from the *middle ear* (which we will discuss later) by the *round window;* the scala vestibuli is closed by the *oval window*. The partition itself is bounded by two membranes, *Reissner's membrane* and the *basilar* membrane, which contain between them the sensory organs whose nerves lead eventually to the central nervous system and the brain. The partition is filled with *endolymph fluid*. The endolymph is the fluid that filled the primitive ear vesicle, and the perilymph is a later addition in the higher vertebrates. Fishes, for instance, have nothing that can properly be called perilymph, but they have no oval or round window either. Apparently there is a connection between having windows and having perilymph, but that is an unsolved question.

The cochlear structure is excited through the oval window by motions of the *stirrup footplate* (a part of the middle ear) acting as a piston. The window is located at the basal or large end of the cochlea. If it is displaced very slowly inward, the incompressible perilymph is displaced toward the apical or small end through the scala vestibuli. There the fluid travels through the apical opening in the partition, called the *helicotrema,* and back on the other side of the partition (scala tympani) to the basal end. At the basal end there is the round window, sealed by a membrane, which moves outward to accommodate the motion of the perilymph.

The vibrations of sound are anything but slow, and the behavior of the inner ear is very different under their influence. To form some conception of this behavior, we can consider the response to a "simple" sound such as a sharp pressure wave, which produces the sensation of a sharp click. When a pressure wave pushes the oval window suddenly inward, the perilymph has no time to travel the long way round through the helicotrema to the round window. Something must give, and what gives is the cochlear partition, which bends or bulges downward into the scala tympani. At first the partition bulges near the basal end, but as time goes on the bulge travels toward the helicotrema and reaches it in about three milliseconds. If the displacement of the oval window is retained, the perilymph eventually flows around through the helicotrema as before. The excitation of the sensory nerve endings distributed along the length of the partition evokes in us the sensation of a click.

If the pressure increase is not so sudden, we hear a "thump" rather than a click. In this case the perilymph has time to flow a bit. The bulge in the partition is broader, and the position of greatest initial deformity lies toward the helicotrema. Thus the bulge

115

travels a shorter distance in equalizing the pressure. The pattern of nerve excitation is different, evoking the sensation of a thump.

We know that the exact dynamics of the traveling wave in the cochlea depend upon the elastic properties of the cochlear partition. This is true not only for the waves excited by clicks and thumps but for all other pressure wave forms as well. It turns out that the direction and shape of the wave motion on the cochlear partition are almost independent of where the partition is excited. This means that if a small hole were drilled in the cochlear wall it could serve as a substitute for the oval window, and the function of the inner ear would be unaltered. This technique is sometimes used to restore hearing when the middle ear path has become inoperative. This fact also explains why we are able to hear sounds by conduction through the bones of the head.

The elastic properties of the cochlear partition are determined principally by the basilar membrane. The other parts merely "ride along," contributing little stiffness or elasticity. As is shown in Fig. 5.7, the

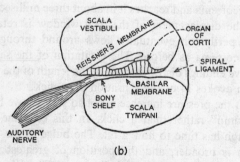

(b)

CROSS SECTION OF COCHLEA

Fig. 5.7

basilar membrane is anchored to a bony shelf extending from the wall of the cochlea on one side; on the other it is attached directly to the cochlear wall by means of a ligament. Near the basal (eardrum) end of the cochlea, the bony shelf is relatively wide and the basilar membrane is correspondingly narrow. At the other end the membrane occupies most of the space between the walls. It is stiffest and least massive at its narrow end, near the oval window, and laxest and most massive at the wide end near the helicotrema. As we might expect, slowly rising thumps tend to deform the membrane nearest the helicotrema, and it takes a sharp click indeed to produce a corresponding deformation in the stiff part. Thus a fast-rising pressure wave or sound wave of high frequency excites the near end; a slow-rising thump or a low-frequency sound wave excites principally the far end.

This kind of direct knowledge concerning a minute, delicate mechanism protected in a nearly inaccessible bony shell comes principally from one man, Georg von Békésy. He has studied the ear for years and has done many extremely ingenious experiments involving direct observation. He reported one classic experiment in the early 1940s. Békésy removed the cochlea from a fresh human cadaver by means of a hollow cylindrical drill. He then attached an electromechanical driving unit to the oval window, so that he could simulate the motion of the stapes and excite the cochlea. By removing part of the cochlear wall, he was able to observe the internal motions with a microscope. He took many precautions; for example, all these operations were carried out under water to avoid drying out the delicate membranes. He performed many auxiliary experiments to confirm his results, and measured the stiffness and the mass of the basilar membrane.

When he excited the oval window, Békésy found that when the basilar membrane is driven into vibration by sine-wave excitation the vibration is strongest

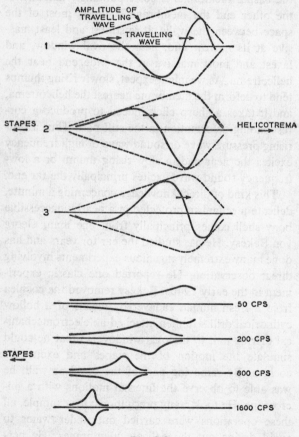

Fig. 5.8

at a particular point on the membrane. It falls off away from this point in either direction but more sharply toward the helicotrema. The greatest vibration is near the oval window for high frequencies, and the point of maximum vibration moves toward the thicker, apical end as the frequency is lowered. As each peak of a sine wave pushes the oval window in, a wave starts down the partition and reaches its maximum amplitude at the place corresponding to the particular frequency being used, then falls away rapidly beyond this point. A picture of such a traveling wave together with the vibration amplitude patterns for several different frequencies is shown in Fig. 5.8. Thus the basilar membrane tends to separate spatially the various frequency components of a stimulating wave. At very low frequencies, below 50 cps, the membrane vibrates as a whole.

The Communicating Hairs

How are these selective vibrations communicated to the nerves? Within the cochlear partition, between

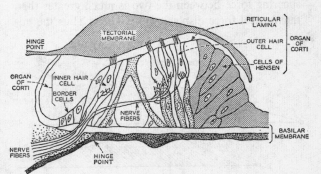

Fig. 5.9

Reissner's membrane and the basilar membrane, in a volume filled with endolymph fluid, lie the sensory organs that tell the brain what is going on at the ear. Fig. 5.7 shows a cross section of the cochlear partition; an enlargement appears in Fig. 5.9. On the basilar membrane lies the *organ of Corti,* which is a collection of fleshy cells. The *tectorial membrane* overlaps the organ of Corti; it acts as though it were hinged (like a window shutter) at a point near the cochlear wall. You will recognize some of the cells in the organ of Corti as *hair cells.* These are known as the *internal* and *external* hair cells, according to their relative positions. There are about 3500 of the former and 20,000 of the latter. The hairs pass through the perforated upper layer of the organ, known as the *reticular lamina,* and are embedded in the tectorial membrane. When the basilar membrane is deformed in vibration, the reticular lamina, tectorial membrane, and organ of Corti slide with respect to each other, bending the hairs. A similar situation is shown in Fig. 5.10 where the relative motion between two sheets hinged at different points is indicated. The shearing force between the two is much greater than the vertical force displacing the sheets. Thus the mi-

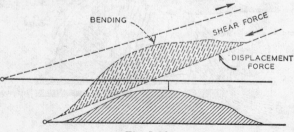

Fig. 5.10

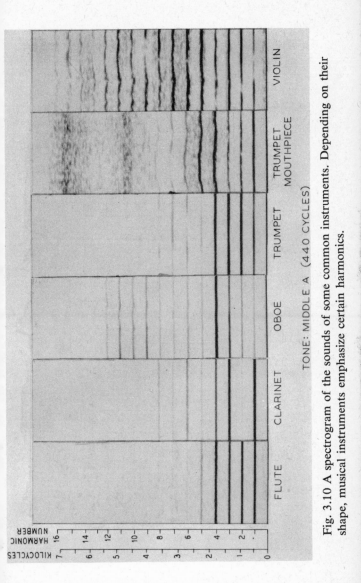

Fig. 3.10 A spectrogram of the sounds of some common instruments. Depending on their shape, musical instruments emphasize certain harmonics.

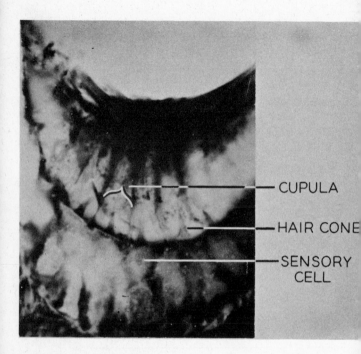

Fig. 5.5b The *tectorial membrane*, one of the many elements in the complex structure of the inner ear of a frog.

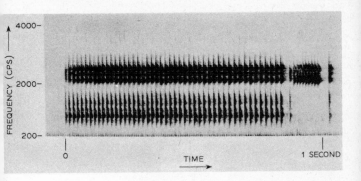

Fig. 7.3 A spectrogram of the sound of *Xenopus,* a South African toad.

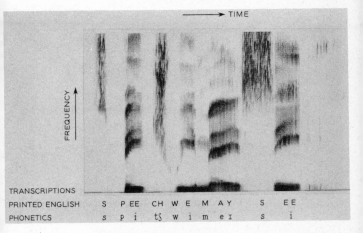

Fig. 7.4 A spectrogram of human speech, depicting the frequency distribution of speech power for successive time intervals.

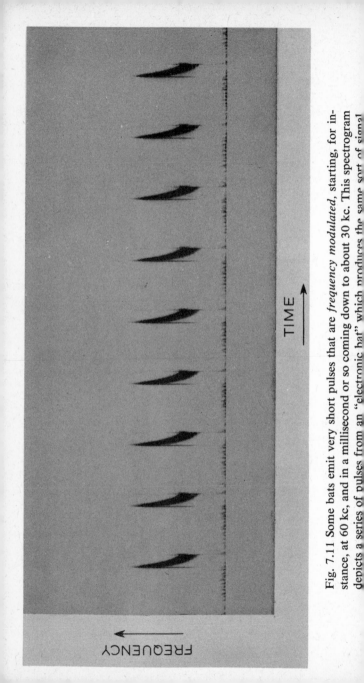

FREQUENCY

TIME

Fig. 7.11 Some bats emit very short pulses that are *frequency modulated*, starting, for instance, at 60 kc, and in a millisecond or so coming down to about 30 kc. This spectrogram depicts a series of pulses from an "electronic bat" which produces the same sort of signal.

nute forces acting on the cochlear partition are multiplied in their effect on the hair cells. This increases the sensitivity of the ear.

We have passed quite painlessly from the anatomy to the physiology of the cochlea; we almost have to, because anatomy is rather dry and uninspiring unless you understand *why* such-and-such a structure is built just that way. For instance, no one had taken particular note of the fact that the tectorial membrane and the basilar membrane were hinged at different points until it was realized that the shear between the two structures was the really interesting force. You can see very readily that the magnitude of the shearing force depends on the distance of the two hinging points.

Now that we have seen how the cochlea operates mechanically, let us return to the basilar papilla of the frog. Here we have no basilar membrane, but only a tectorial membrane. Moreover, if the cochlea is a small structure to look at in detail, then the basilar papilla is truly diminutive.

In the big frog, such as a bullfrog, the longest dimension of the cartilage ring is a little more than ½ millimeter, or $\frac{2}{100}$ inch. The tectorial membrane is about half as large across. All that is known at present about the mechanics of that membrane has been learned from enlarged artificial models, and we must hope that the modeling was accurate enough. The tectorial membrane has a peculiar variation in elasticity, which allows, just as does the basilar membrane of the cochlea, for waves to travel on it and reach maxima of amplitude at different places, according to the frequency of the wave. Fig. 5.11a shows the elastic pattern of the tectorial membrane. The very dark areas are stiff, and the very light areas are lax. You can see the gradual change in stiffness. In Fig. 5.11b are illustrated envelopes of the waves on the membrane as the result of high frequency stimulation; as you see, there are two of them, because the membrane is symmetrical. Fig. 5.11c shows the wave pattern envelope in a low-frequency stimulus. Note that the maximum has moved farther down than in Fig. 5.11b. Now it also becomes apparent what function the *central mass* serves: it "squeezes" the wave motion toward the cartilage ring, where the sensory cells are. Their hairs are moved by the motions of the membrane directly, without intervention of the shear

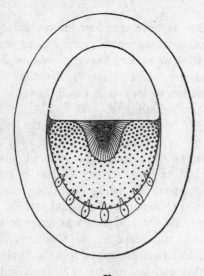

a

Fig. 5.11a

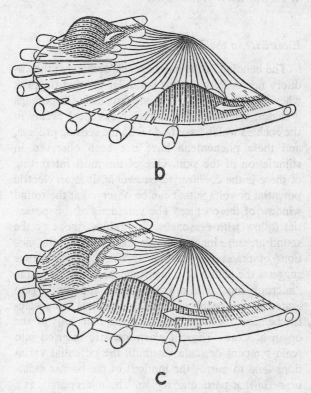

Fig. 5.11b, c

mechanism we saw in the cochlea. You see, it is the *relative* motion of two structures that counts, and since in the basilar papilla the hair cells are firmly fixed in the cartilage ring, moving the membrane is sufficient. But in the cochlea the hair cells (on the basilar membrane) and the tectorial membrane move *together* and relative motion is only possible by some assymetrical arrangement that causes shear.

Electricity in the Ear

The bending of the hairs excites, somehow, the auditory nerve. Perhaps this is similar to what happens when the hairs on the arm are brushed. Or perhaps it is not, for there are particular electrical events in the cochlea which have to do with the sensing process, and these phenomena have not been observed in stimulation of the skin. One of the most interesting of these is the *cochlear microphonic*. It is an electric potential or voltage that can be observed at the round window of the cochlea. The variations of this potential follow with reasonable faithfulness those of the sound pressure incident on the ear (actually, the motions of the stapes footplate). This correspondence suggests the action of a microphone, hence the name "microphonic." The microphonic is apparently generated in the cochlea. It probably arises from electrochemical reactions involving the hair cells of the organ of Corti. Thus, if electrodes are inserted into scala tympani or scala vestibuli, the potential variations tend to mirror the motions of the basilar membrane in that particular region. The microphonic is a handy phenomenon for studying the ear since it is a built-in microphone through which the vibrations of the middle ear and cochlea can be observed.

Indeed, I recently witnessed a demonstration in which this effect in a cat's ear provided the microphone for a public-address system. A surgically implanted electrode was in contact with the cat's round window. This electrode was attached to the input of a small, battery-operated amplifier held on the animal's collar. The amplified output fed the public-address system just as a microphone would. The speaker captured the cat, which had previously been walking about normally, and spoke into its ear. The microphone voltage picked up by the electrode provided a rather high-quality speech signal for the audience of acousticians.

At high sound levels, above 80 db, the microphonic intensity no longer increases with intensity of the stimulus but tends to remain constant or even to decrease slightly. At such high sound levels another potential, called the *summating potential,* begins to appear. It is slowly changing compared to the microphonic; it would, for instance, follow the intensity variations in speech. That is, it would be large on a loud vowel and small on weak consonants. The summating potential which is observed depends upon where in the cochlea it is measured. At some points loud sounds may produce a large decrease in voltage. In other words, the summating potential can be positive or negative in effect.

The cochlear microphonic is closely associated with the hair cells. When they are removed, the microphonic disappears. It may be that the summating potential has a similar origin, but this has not been established. Békésy found that the microphonic is produced by shearing action on the hair cells. It could be that at high sound levels a constant shear displacement between the tectorial membrane and the reticular lamina leads to the summating potential. But this idea is pure speculation. The source of the summating potential is yet to be proved.

Certainly, though, both potentials are true physiological responses and not artifices of the experimental method. Such a response implies a triggering action in which energy stored in the nervous system is released.

One possible source of such energy is the so-called *endolymphatic potential,* which is a steady voltage that can be measured between the endolymph inside the cochlear partition and the perilymph outside. This potential is maintained by metabolic activity somewhere nearby in the cochlea. A steady voltage of this kind stores energy, which can be released by a triggering mechanism.

Some Intriguing Questions

Actually the function of these electrical phenomena in hearing is not at all a settled question. Inevitably, though, there have been speculations. For instance, if an electronic engineer were asked, "What is it that has a steady supply voltage and a fluctuating output proportional to input except at high input levels?" he would immediately answer, "An amplifier." Indeed, Dr. Hallowell Davis of St. Louis' Central Institute for the Deaf has suggested that the potentials may be evidences of a biological electromechanical amplifier. Conceivably the chain of events might be: shearing motions on the hair cells are converted to an electrical voltage and amplified in the process; this voltage then excites the nerve endings which lead eventually to the brain. However beguiling this notion may be, its validity must rest upon evidence not yet in hand.

A naive interpretation of the microphonic is the "telephone theory" of hearing, according to which one presumes that a transmission line runs from ear to brain—with the ear serving merely as a microphone. There is little support in physiology for such a view.

In fact, it rather reminds one of the sort of explanation of the cosmos in which the earth is supported by four elephants which themselves stand on the back of a tortoise, which stands on what? In the microphonic theory of hearing the need for explanation is merely pushed further away from the ear.

The microphonic potential, however, is not an exclusive property of the cochlea; it is found in all the maculae of the inner ear, even those that have nothing to do with hearing, such as the maculae of the semicircular canals and the utricle. The lateral line organ generates beautiful microphonic potentials—and even a summating potential. The people who work with these organs prefer to speak of "generator potentials" because "microphonic" is much too suggestive of sound, and there is no good evidence that the lateral line organ has anything to do with sound. The semicircular canals clearly have no relation whatever to sound (they measure angular acceleration); yet they show generator potentials and can be stimulated by sound! Dr. J. Tonndorf of the State University of Iowa blasted a deaf man with a loud sound; although the man heard nothing, he became profoundly dizzy (dizziness is caused mostly by malfunction of the semicircular canals). This is a very nice demonstration of the fact that although you may be able to obtain a response to sounds for some organ, you may not conclude that the organ is therefore a hearing organ. The situation may even be worse: suppose you wished to find out whether fishes hear. You could look at the ear, and insert electrodes to study microphonics or even nerve discharges. But, as we saw, that is not a foolproof method. You could then proceed to train the fish to do something, say come to a feeding station, when you produce a sound. Assume that you are successful and even get an audiogram or threshold curve (see Chapter IV); does that prove that the fish hears? It would appear that it does. In fact, the experiment has often been performed and the conclusion dutifully drawn.

But . . .

Fishes are also very easily trained to come for food with small changes in atmospheric pressure as the stimulus. Recently I obtained some (though incomplete and still *very* debatable) evidence that at least tadpoles—and perhaps fishes—perceive static pressure by the frequency of a vibration produced in their own lungs or swim bladders. They would, if this were true, perceive sounds as *pressure*. The conclusion that they hear would be comparable to saying that Tonndorf's patient heard, because he became dizzy. The trouble with experiments on animals is that you cannot ask them questions; you have to think of experiments which, in fact, ask your questions in a "language" the animal understands. The incompleteness of the fragments of knowledge we have about animals' perception is eloquent testimony of the difficulty.

Waves in the Cochlea

Let us return to old reliable mankind and the processes in the cochlea. The sensory effects of all the electrical and mechanical activity that goes on in the cochlea have been illustrated very graphically in a model built by Békésy. He used plastic to cover a narrow longitudinal slit in a brass tube, as shown in Fig. 5.12. The plastic along the slit is tapered in thick-

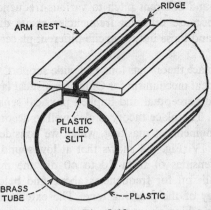

Fig. 5.12

ness and raised into a ridge. The tube is filled with water, one end being closed by a plate, the other by a piston. The elasticity of the plastic-filled slit changes along its length just as the elasticity of the cochlear partition does. Thus the two structures tend to vibrate in a similar way. If an observer places his arm in contact with the ridge, he can feel that, as the frequency of the signal driving the piston is changed over its permissible range (about 40 to 150 cps), the position of maximum stimulation moves from one end of the model to the other. Of course, the sensation is not one of "pitch," but the process is similar in many respects to that by which motion of the basilar membrane is sensed.

This notion of cochlear action leads to what has been called the "place" theory of hearing. According to the place theory, the psychical quantity pitch is directly related to a place co-ordinate in the cochlea and perhaps in the brain. For example, we assign a

129

distinct and different pitch to various-frequency sine waves because different frequencies excite different nerves, and these in turn excite different places in the brain.

The place theory has long had wide support. It provides a neat mechanism for Ohm's acoustical law with its stated perceptual and implied physical separation of tones. The place theory is also well in accord with the phenomena of masking, which we considered in Chapter IV. Fig. 4.8 shows that at low sound levels with intensities of from 20 to 40 db, the masking effect falls off for frequencies above and below the frequency of the masking tone. The extent and degree of masking above the masking frequency can be explained in terms of the extent and degree of vibration of the basilar membrane away from the point of maximum excitation for the masking frequency. Consider the "critical bandwidths." You will recall that a noise must fall within a certain bandwidth about a tone if the noise is to exert a masking effect on the tone; and that within a larger bandwidth the loudness of two tones of different frequency is not the sum of their separate loudness. These "critical bandwidths" we can think of in terms of how the excitation produced by one of the tones of one particular frequency spreads along the basilar membrane.

More intense tones tend to mask tones of higher frequency. We can well imagine that an intense tone strongly shakes all the cochlear partition between the oval window, where the cochlea is excited, and the point of maximum vibration, but that the disturbance does not travel beyond this point to the portions of the cochlea which are excited by low frequencies.

The beats observed at harmonic frequencies in Fig.

4.8 we explain by saying that at high sound levels the vibration of the middle and inner ear is non-linear. Such non-linear motion will produce harmonic components of vibration which, in all their effects, will be like harmonic frequencies introduced into the ear from outside.

Harvey Fletcher studied the masking effects a noise containing a wide range of frequencies has on tones of various frequencies. By making some simple and plausible assumptions, he was able to deduce the position of maximum excitation along the basilar membrane corresponding to each frequency. Thus he obtained a curve showing position of maximum excitation in relation to frequency. It was not based on direct observation of the cochlea but on a knowledge of the general function of the membrane, an assumption that each millimeter of its length has the same number of nerve endings, and on masking data. Fletcher's curve agrees very well with Békésy's observations of the position of the point of maximum excitation for each frequency!

Surely all this seems strong evidence in favor of the place theory of hearing. It certainly shows at least that a place phenomenon is involved in hearing. There is, however, evidence that the place theory is at best incomplete.

One argument against a simple "inner-ear" place theory is concerned with man's high degree of frequency discrimination. In sound with a frequency of 1000 cycles we can detect frequency changes of less than 1 per cent. Localization of the vibration on the basilar membrane for the various frequencies seems not nearly sharp enough to account for this degree of acuity. Further, our sense of pitch persists down to a range of frequencies that all attain their maxima of vibration right at the helicotrema. Our sense of pitch is based on more than just the separation of tone waves on the basilar membrane. Apparently there must be some "pitch-sharpening" mechanism in the neural pathways in and beyond the cochlea.

Interestingly, Békésy found such a mechanism in his model experiments using the skin of the arm. Even though the vibration of his plastic basilar membrane showed a very broad pattern with only an ill-defined maximum, the sensations on the skin were localized to a very narrow region. These relations are shown in Fig. 5.13. Evidently the vibrations near the maximum were the only ones "getting through" via the nerve pathways; the others were inhibited by the "sharpening" or "funneling" mechanism.

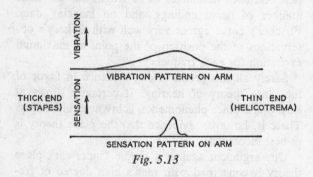

Fig. 5.13

The foregoing observations do not invalidate place theory in the broad sense; they do require that nerve elements in and beyond the inner ear be brought into play to account for man's pitch acuity. There is, however, strong evidence against a pure place theory of hearing even when the neural elements are considered.

Under some conditions we hear a subjective pitch corresponding to a section of the basilar membrane that is not vibrating at all! This is known as the *residue phenomenon* of Schouten, an ingenious contemporary Dutch acoustician. It may occur when a musical tone whose fundamental component has been removed is presented to the ear.

We remember that the tone of an organ pipe consists of a fundamental frequency and many overtones. It has been found that the subjective pitch of such a complex of tones is the same as that of the fundamental whether that component—the fundamental itself —is present or not. Moreover, the sense of the pitch of such a tone persists even when a strong low-frequency masking noise is present, a noise that would mask the fundamental frequency if it were present or in some way generated in the ear. Thus we hear a pitch whose "place" is not excited—nor, of course, are the corresponding nerves. This appears to leave a "pure" place theory in a bad way.

It is clear from quite other considerations that there must be more to hearing than the place theory encompasses. From the foregoing discussion we can easily understand the beats we hear when two tones close together in frequency are presented to the same ear: the cochlea vibrates with a varying intensity, in accord with the beating of the two waves, as in Fig. 4.7. However, most people hear beats when we excite one ear with a tone of one frequency and the other ear with a tone of a slightly different frequency. Such *binaural beats* cannot be explained by a mechanical motion of the cochlea. Neither can the facts of binaural localization.

It appears that there is much to the phenomena of

hearing that lies beyond the fine and ingenious mechanism of the inner ear. The inner ear plays a part in distilling from the complex sounds reaching our ears the distinct sensations of which we are aware. But there is more to the analysis of sound than what we find in the mechanical function of the basilar membrane. The nervous system and the brain play a part as well.

The Outer Ear

The inner ear, as we have seen, is filled with fluid. For creatures that live in air, this presents a problem. As we saw earlier, sound waves are reflected from solid walls; the oval window and the perilymph are solid walls for airborne sound. Very little of the energy impinging on the ear would ever penetrate to excite the hair cells, were it not that Nature has provided animals with various *auxiliary organs* to take care of this difficulty. The *outer* and *middle ear* are the structures that take care of *matching* the two systems, air and fluid.

Birds, as we saw, have no outwardly visible ear. But at least you can find an opening in the bird's head which corresponds to the opening you find in the center of your own ear. This hole is the open end of a tube, called the *meatus* or *ear canal*. The other end is closed by the *eardrum,* as illustrated in Fig. 5.14. The sometimes-present *pinna,* as the outwardly visible (and in most animals movable) ear flap is called, together with the meatus, form the *outer* ear. Frogs, as we saw in Chapter I, and many other animals have no outer ears at all. Some animals, notably insects, do not have ears in their heads but in such un-

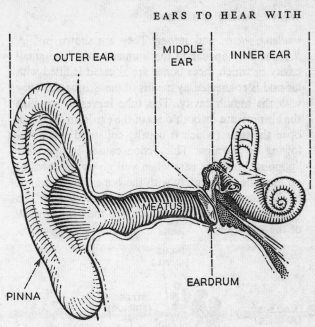

Fig. 5.14

likely places as legs (some crickets) or the thorax, the "middle" portion of the insect body to which the legs attach (some grasshoppers).

On the other side of the eardrum—that is, the inside —we find, depending again on what species of animal we look at, one, two, or three very small and light bones, the so-called middle ear bones or *ossicles*. Reptiles such as alligators and birds have a single rod-like bone, which looks like a column and is appropriately called a *columella*. Most frogs have two bones, which sometimes grow together into one, but all mammals have three. They are called *hammer, anvil,* and *stirrup;* or, since anatomists like to use Latin to avoid being misunderstood by foreign readers, *malleus, incus,* and *stapes*. They are shown in Fig. 5.15 as they appear in the human being. The small cavity in which these bones are situated is filled with air and is connected by means of the *Eustachian tube* with the mouth cavity. This tube serves to equalize the air pressure on both sides of the eardrum. You can open the tube (which is usually collapsed) by swallowing or yawning. This action causes the peculiar "popping" of your ears when you go up or down in an airplane. The cavity with the bones and entrance of the Eustachian tube is called the *middle ear*. The footplate of the stapes is attached to the *oval window* of the *inner ear*.

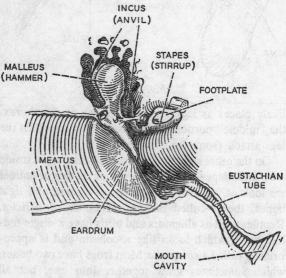

Fig. 5.15

So much for the anatomy; let us now look at the functions of these organs.

The external meatus is somewhat like an organ pipe, open at the ear-lobe end and closed with a nearly rigid wall at the drum. The average length of the canal is around 2.7 centimeters, about one inch. If it acted exactly like an open pipe its lowest resonant frequency would be $1130/4L = 3390$ cycles per second. Near this resonant frequency, the distribution of sound pressure would be as shown for the pipe of Fig. 3.8. The pressure would be very high at the left end, corresponding to the eardrum, but very low at the right open end, which is excited by the sound.

In actual fact the eardrum is not as perfectly rigid as the end of the organ pipe. Further, the canal flares to a larger area near the open end. For these reasons the actual pressure distribution is not precisely that of Fig. 3.8. The ratio of the pressure at the closed eardrum end to the pressure at the open ear-lobe end is not as high as it would be for a straight, rigid tube. Nonetheless, the external meatus does function as a resonator. Its resonant frequency corresponds closely to the frequency of greatest acuity of hearing, as given in Fig. 4.1. Near this frequency the pressure at the eardrum is considerably higher than the pressure at the external ear, which latter, because of reflection or shadowing by the head, is itself lower or higher than the "free-field" pressure of a sound wave.

The meatus, in fact, supplies a pressure amplification of between 5 and 10 db over the range from 2000 to 5500 cycles per second. In this frequency range our hearing would be less acute by that amount if the eardrum were at the surface of the head. At lower frequencies the pressure amplification is less, and at very low frequencies the pressure at the eardrum is the same as the pressure of the sound wave impinging on the ear.

The meatus has other functions. Among these is protection of the temperature and the humidity at the eardrum, whose elastic characteristics change radically with these conditions. Because the drum is sheltered by the meatus, both temperature and humidity at the drum are relatively independent of environmental conditions.

The Middle Ear

The eardrum marks the boundary between the outer and the middle ear. It is at this point that acoustic pressure variations are changed or transformed into mechanical motion. The pressure wave at the inner end of the meatus forces the eardrum into a sympathetic vibration. The displacement of the drum from its rest position during such vibrations is incredibly small. For the sounds encountered in ordinary conversation the displacement is about the same as the diameter of a hydrogen molecule, or 10^{-8} (1/100,000,000) centimeter.

It is the function of the middle ear to transmit the eardrum's motions to the inner ear, where they excite the auditory nerve. The actual mechanics of vibration of this bony chain are quite complex. There is not as yet general agreement among physiologists about its detailed motions. Functionally, however, there is no doubt that it operates as shown in Fig. 5.16a. Inward motions of the eardrum are transmitted as reduced and more forcible inward motions of the stapes footplate.

In transmitting vibrations from the eardrum to the

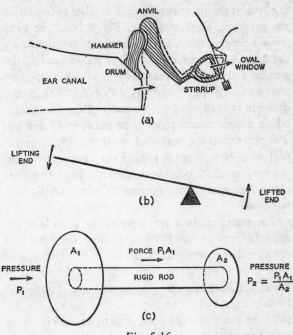

Fig. 5.16

inner ear, the middle ear performs two important transformations. First it changes the relatively large motions at the drum to motions at the middle ear which are about 1.3 to 3 times smaller. This action is much like that of a lever used to lift a heavy load, as shown in Fig. 5.16b. Typically, the lifting end of the lever is forced through a greater distance than the lifted end. This is the price paid for the lever's "mechanical advantage," which enables the operator to move a very heavy load by applying only a moderate force.

The second transformation arises because the driving area at the inner ear is much smaller than that of the eardrum, as illustrated in Fig. 5.16c. The total force acting at the left is the pressure multiplied by the area A. This total force, F, is transmitted to the smaller end where the pressure is the force divided by the area A_2, or $P_2 = F/A_2 = P_1A_1/A_2$. Thus the pressure is multiplied by the ratio of the two areas, which measurements show to be between 15 and 30. The pressure at the oval window—that is, the force per unit area—is very much greater than the pressure on the eardrum both because of the lever action and because the larger eardrum drives the much smaller oval window.

The effect of these transformations is to increase the efficiency of energy transfer from the light and compressible external air to the dense and incompressible fluid (perilymph) with which the inner ear is filled. We have seen that a sound wave is reflected from a rigid wall. The oval window backed by the perilymph is quite rigid compared to air, and it would reflect most of the incident sound energy were it not for the matching action of the middle ear. Only through this means is the ear able to sense the minute amounts of energy carried by the sounds of everyday life.

In addition to its function of transmitting and transforming vibration, the middle ear defends us against loud noises and extreme vibrations. The ossicles are so suspended by their various muscles that they are free to vibrate in more than one manner or mode. The dominant mode is shown in Fig. 5.16. When excitation of the eardrum becomes too severe, the ossicles shift to a second mode of vibration. The distinction between these two modes lies chiefly in the motion of the stapes. Ordinarily the stapes rotates about an axis at one end of the footplate and perpendicular to it. In protecting the inner ear against high sound intensities it rotates about an axis lying through and parallel to the footplate, at right angles to the first mode. Thus its net effect on the inner ear is materially reduced.

Two small muscles, one associated with the eardrum, the other with the stapes, provide a second protective mechanism. In a reflex response to loud sounds the first pulls the drum inward, increasing its stiffness, while the second displaces the stapes and decreases its coupling to the inner ear. These reflex actions seem to be analogous to the regulatory action of the iris, which protects the eye against intense light.

Unfortunately, neither of the ear's protective devices is capable of fast adaptation. Sudden, extremely intense noises can do permanent damage. In this category of sounds are gunfire and the shock waves from explosions. Some of the sensory nerves of the inner ear are particularly sensitive to damage. In persons who have been exposed to intense sounds we typically find hearing loss at frequencies near 4000 cycles per second. The nerves responsible for the hearing in this range are perhaps particularly vulnerable.

The picture we have drawn of the function of the middle ear applies only for comparatively low frequencies, below 3000 or 4000 cycles per second. At higher frequencies the functional behavior is altered in detail. For instance, in its usual state the eardrum is pulled inward somewhat by the muscles of the middle ear, forming it into a conical shape much like that of a loudspeaker cone. In the same manner as such a cone, the drum moves very nearly as a unit at low frequencies. At higher frequencies, however, it "breaks up" and vibrates in sections, thereby altering its effective area. Nevertheless, the function is different not in kind but only in degree.

Out of all the work we have described in this chapter, out of the efforts of anatomists, physiologists, acousticians, and psychologists, has come some understanding. But before we pride ourselves on our knowledge, it might be well to realize how incomplete that knowledge is. In dealing with the acoustics and mechanics of the various parts of the ear we are on reasonably secure ground, although many of the details are obscure. We know very little about the way in which the mechanical events in the cochlea are translated into electrical events by the hair cells, although we have in the microphonic potential a wonderful tool for monitoring the process. About the production of nerve impulses we do know a considerable amount, as you will see in the next chapter, but most of the work to be discussed was done on nerves considerably larger than the ultra-fine fibers that innervate the ear; we have to make some plausible assumptions if we want to apply it to the action of the cochlear nerves. The connections of the auditory nerves to the brain have been traced in part, but the functional aspects of that vast and complicated network are ill understood. When it comes to the hearing of creatures other than ourselves, we know something of the mammals, because they are equipped with ears very much like ours; from the birds on down the evolutionary scale, however, our knowledge is fragmentary and debatable.

In all, then, the depth and precision of our understanding lessen as we direct our consideration from the external ear step by step inward to the brain, and from the human down into the animal kingdom. Of our understanding of the process of hearing as a whole we can say only that we have some facts, some speculation which takes us a little way beyond these, and a great area of obscurity, which involves the little-understood functioning of the central nervous system and the brain.

CHAPTER VI

Nerves and the Brain

Somewhere, somehow, in that great raveled knot within our skulls, we live, we hear, we see, we are conscious of our being. There, in some sort of physical reality, are all those subjective phenomena—those sensations of taste, color, and of the timbre of sounds—which Galileo once ruled out of the province of natural science. We still do not understand these matters. Science is not, however, content with knowing the external world, or the purely mechanical properties of the body; it will not call a halt at either the complicated linkages of our limbs or the subtle motions of the basilar membrane. In tracing out our understanding of hearing we must travel along the nerves that connect the inner ear to the brain and on into the brain itself. What alternatives present themselves?

The cables by which the ear communicates with the brain are chains of cells known as *neurons* or nerve cells. To the body of each cell is attached a long thin extension known as the *axon,* which terminates in a nerve ending or *terminal arbor,* as shown in Fig. 6.1. Each connection to a subsequent neuron is made

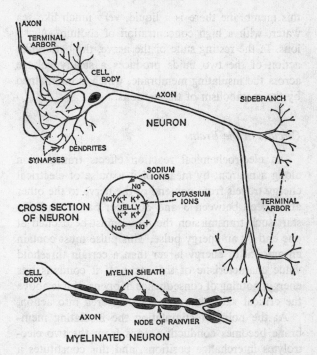

Fig. 6.1

through a *synapse*, which is merely a name for the connecting point.

The nerve has a significant concentric structure, shown in Fig. 6.1. The innermost layer is a jellylike substance containing a high concentration of potassium (K^+) ions. (*Ions* are atoms which have lost or acquired electrons, thereby taking on an electric charge.) This structure is surrounded by a sheath and a membrane which gives the nerve its mechanical strength and acts as an electrical insulator. Outside

145

this membrane there is a liquid, very much like sea water, with a high concentration of sodium (Na^+) ions. In the resting state of the nerve, the batterylike action of the two fluids produces a steady voltage across the insulating membrane, which is maintained by the metabolism of the neurons.

Circuits in the Brain

An electrochemical reaction effects transmission along a neuron; by means of it a pulse of electrical energy travels from one end of the nerve to the other at a speed between 3 and 300 feet per second. To start such transmission the nerve must be excited at one end by an energy pulse. This pulse must contain an amount of energy larger than a certain threshold value characteristic of the nerve. If it contains less energy, nothing of consequence happens. If it is above the critical value, the nerve is triggered into action.

At the point of stimulation the insulating membrane becomes conducting. Ions from the two electrolytes interchange positions, and this constitutes a current flow. The action is self-sustaining. A sort of "smoke ring" of current proceeds down the axon. Most of the current flow is in a direction transverse to the direction in which the pulse travels. After passage of the pulse, the nerve cannot be fired for a period of the order of 1 to 3 milliseconds (thousandths of a second), but shortly thereafter it returns to its normal resting state. This "dead" period, during which the nerve recuperates by moving the K^+ and Na^+ ions back where they were before the impulse passed, is called the *refractory period*.

The velocity of the pulse depends upon the diameter of the nerve: the larger it is, the faster the propagation. Neurons in primitive animals such as the squid come in sizes up to 0.1 inch in diameter. Even here the velocity is slow, of the order of a few feet per second. Higher forms of life, such as man, would have a difficult time indeed if communication between parts of the body took a second or more. Think of one of the long single neurons connecting the foot to the spinal cord and thence via synapses to other nerves and the brain. How difficult it would be to climb a flight of stairs in the dark if seconds intervened between the placing of the foot and the sensing that it is there.

Nature has provided a mechanism for increasing the speed of nerve transmission. In human beings and most mammals we find the nerve axons coated with an electrical insulator called *myelin*. This coating is interrupted periodically along the axon by nodes (the *nodes of Ranvier*) where the nerve membrane is exposed. When a nerve impulse travels along such a *myelinated* nerve, the "smoke ring" of current jumps from one node to the next, thereby effectively speeding the propagation. Velocities up to 300 feet per second have been measured. We might look upon these myelinated nerves which permit fast reactions as a great advance in the technology of life. They make their appearance high on the evolutionary scale and are evidently a recent development.

As an axon approaches a synaptic connection it divides into many small branches (see Fig. 6.1). This *terminal arbor* makes contact with similar growths, called the *dendrites,* from the succeeding cell body. These small branches have no myelin sheath. Thus the nerve pulse is delayed in its travel. The actual transfer of activity across the connection, from terminal arbor to the dendrites of the succeeding cell body, is not well understood. It may be that this is entirely an electrical process; but there are those who believe that it is accomplished by the secretion of an excitatory chemical. That each neuron excites a succeeding one, with an associated *latency* or delay, there can be no doubt.

The peripheral nerve twigs that make contact with the sensory cells of the ear are really modified dendrites that apparently behave like axons. Actually, the contact between the hair cells and the nerve twigs is a sort of synapse.

The nerve pulse has a standard shape, regardless of the nature of the excitation. This is somewhat as shown in Fig. 6.2. Thus nerves have two states only,

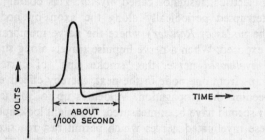

NERVE PULSE

Fig. 6.2

active or inactive. One often hears the statement that neurons are off-on devices. This means that an *individual nerve pulse* cannot carry information about the intensity of a stimulus but only about whether a stimulus of sufficient energy is present or not.

Nevertheless, neurons respond to intensity. The number of firings in a given time interval increases as the intensity rises. Thus the nervous system "codes" intensity into frequency. But there is a limit to this correspondence. It arises because two successive firings of a nerve fiber must ordinarily be separated by about $\frac{1}{300}$ second (refractory period). Therefore the maximum rate of discharge is around 300 pulses per second. Once a nerve fiber reaches its maximum rate, further increase in the stimulus intensity has no effect.

The Mechanics of Loudness

We are called upon to discriminate among a tremendous range of intensities in our sensory activity; it is much greater than the range of some hundreds to one that a single nerve fiber, firing at different rates under different intensities of stimulation, can cover. Nature is ingenious. To connect our sensory organs to the central nervous system she provided many neurons in parallel, making nerve bundles or *nerves,* for short. The *threshold values* of the various neurons forming a nerve cover a wide range of intensities, allowing the nerve as a whole to respond selectively to a much broader range than can any neuron individually.

Moreover, the particular way in which the nerve fibers terminate among the inner and outer hair cells quite probably has something to do with this. Fig. 6.3 shows a small section from a turn of the cochlea; the view is that looking down on the basilar membrane from the top of the snail shell. In the "core" of the shell (see also Fig. 6.4) are situated the cell bodies

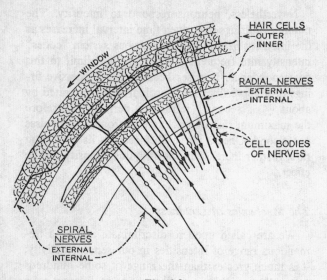

Fig. 6.3

of the sensory nerves; their modified dendrites emerge and course in various ways to the hair cells. We find *radial nerves,* which come out like spokes of a wheel and connect to single inner or outer hair cells. Then there are the *spiral nerves,* which run for some length parallel to the perimeter of the cochlea, and make contact with many hair cells by means of side branches. The outer or external spiral fibers are sensory fibers; the internal spiral fibers are probably not sensory, but carry impulses toward the hair cells, rather than away from them as the other nerves do. The radial fibers connect mostly to the inner hair cells, while the external spiral ones connect only to outer hair cells. Since the external spiral fibers connect to many hair cells over a considerable stretch of the

150

cochlea (as much as a third of a turn), they gather information from many places along the cochlea at once, while the radial fibers can transmit signals only when something happens at the precise spot where they terminate. This has led people to think that the spiral innervation is a sort of "integrator," which puts together bits and pieces of information that are scattered around in the cochlea. Recently, however, it has become possible to construct small electronic devices that simulate neuron functions. With such devices one could imitate the spiral innervation and see if it really worked as an integrator. When I did such an experiment, I was surprised to find that it did not—at least not in the way people had thought it would. It turns out that the spiral innervation is a trick Nature uses to extend the range of intensities we can hear. A single neuron can handle about 20 db, or a hundredfold increase of intensity between just threshold firing and its maximum rate. When I made an artificial spiral fiber with ten side-branches, I found that it could handle a 40-db, or ten-thousandfold increase in intensity.

You see now that there are two different ways in which the intensity range of the ear may be extended: through many different threshold values of the neurons, and through nerve fibers with many side branches. Which way Nature uses is not yet clear; very possibly both, or perhaps even a third way we have not yet dreamed of.

Fletcher proposed a theory of subjective loudness on the basis of these properties of nerves. He said that loudness may be proportional to the total number of nerve impulses produced per second: If a sound is made twice as loud in sones, it must excite the nerves to send out pulses at twice the rate.

This is certainly in accord with the ideas concerning subjective loudness which went into the construction of the loudness scale of Fig. 4.3. A sound heard by both ears will produce twice as many nerve impulses as the same sound heard by one ear alone. In addition, separate tones far enough apart in frequency will produce nerve impulses almost independently, since they are resolved individually by the basilar membrane. Two such tones of equal loudness should together give a sound twice as loud as either alone, and ten equally loud tones should together give a sound ten times as loud as any individual tone.

Truly to test Fletcher's theory, however, experiment would have to show that as we make a particular sound wave more intense the subjective loudness corresponds to the total number of nerve discharges per second. We would have to know how the thresholds of stimulation are distributed among the nerves of a patch of nerve endings in the ear. These data are not available, but an outstanding physiologist, Selig Hecht, studied the distribution of threshold levels among the nerve cells of the eye. By assuming that the nerves of the ear behave in a like manner, Fletcher was able to compute a curve of total rate of nerve discharges against loudness level; it is in fair agreement with Fig. 4.3, the experimental relation between subjective loudness in sones and loudness level in phons.

There is some indication that the size of the *limen,* or least noticeable difference of loudness, can be explained, for a part of the loudness range, at least, in terms of statistical variations in the excitation of nerve pulses by sound, providing we assume with Fletcher that loudness is proportional to number of nerve pulses per second.

This sort of speculation about loudness is illustrative of auditory theory, whose aim is to explain sensation (for example, loudness) in physical or mechanical terms (for example, counting the number of pulses per second). Of course, sounds can evoke many sensations—loudness, timbre or color, pitch, etc. —but traditionally pitch has occupied a pre-eminent position in auditory theory. We have seen that the "pitch-place" theory explains many facts of audition —but leaves others unexplained. When we consider the anatomy of neural hearing circuits, what alternative is possible? How can the phenomena of binaural hearing, and the other sensations described in Chapter IV, be accounted for?

The answers to these questions must involve the neural connection from the organ of Corti to the central nervous system, for all auditory information must pass over this path—that is, over the auditory nerve. They must also involve the pathways in the central nervous system, which eventually connect the auditory nerve to the cortex. These pathways, composed of many tens of thousands of neurons, are extremely complex. But amid this complexity a certain order is discernible.

The Auditory Nerve

The cochlea is innervated by the auditory nerve, which contains some 30,000 individual neurons. The nerve runs down the center of the cochlea, spiraling in conformity with the turns. To serve the entire length of the cochlea, neurons break away from the main bundle continuously along the way. They penetrate the cochlear partition into the organ of Corti, where they come in close proximity to the hair cells, as shown in Figs. 6.3 and 6.4.

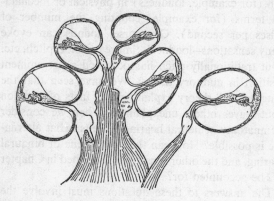

Fig. 6.4

The auditory nerve enters the central nervous system and its neurons end amid a concentrated mass of cell bodies. This mass is known as the *cochlear nucleus*. We might consider this a way station in the auditory pathway. It is a place where purposeful synaptic interconnections are made. Some of the outgoing neurons from this mass extend upward to another way station of cell bodies called the *inferior colliculus*. Others pass through various way stations in the lower brain stem, and some interconnect with similar ones from the opposite ear. Thus the two ears are first linked at a level low in the auditory tract. The upward-going neurons from the inferior colliculus terminate in the *medial geniculate body,* whose axons in turn lead directly to the "auditory" regions of the cortex. These are situated symmetrically along the sides of the brain. While this is by far the best-known path from ear to brain, it is not the only one. Evidence for at least two other ascending, parallel paths has been found. Possibly along each of these paths different tasks are performed on the neural data passing through it. In addition, the neurons appear to be connected in both one-to-one and many-to-one relation. The nervous system has many strings to its bow.

Recent research has found paths descending to lower centers in opposition to the classical ascending ones. These descending neural paths have not been mapped in detail, but there is some evidence that such "feed-back" loops exist all the way from the cortex to the cochlea. Perhaps the brain can communicate with the ear as well as the other way round. The *internal spiral* fibers in the cochlea are probably the termination of this feed-back loop.

The complexity of the auditory tract increases as it ascends. Twice as many axons leave the cochlear nucleus as end upon it. The number—30,000—of auditory-nerve neurons is multiplied some 30 times at least in the number of their extensions ultimately entering the cortex.

What a task physiologists have in trying to learn about the organization of this monster machine! Their task might be likened to that of an engineer who, having only some rudimentary knowledge about the functioning of individual electric circuits, has to draw an organization diagram of one of the large-scale digital computers, popularly described as electronic brains. Picture his confusion when he first looks inside at the array of interacting tubes and multicolored components, many thousand more than you find in your TV set. In these terms, it is remarkable that even the present modest understanding of hearing has been achieved.

The function of all this complex anatomy is little understood. Electrophysiologists have measured in guinea pigs, dogs, cats, and monkeys the electrical impulses excited by carefully measured acoustic stimuli, using electrodes inserted in various parts of the auditory pathway. The animal is usually, but not always, under anesthesia during such measurements. Sometimes semi-permanent electrodes are implanted surgically in various parts of the animal's anatomy. After the animals recover from their operation, the protruding electrodes provide access for observing the electrical events occurring inside.

Another technique for studying the functions of the nervous system is known as *extirpation*. Here "pre-operative" hearing is compared with hearing after a portion of the auditory tract has been surgically removed or otherwise expunged. After the subject recovers from the operation, psychoacoustic tests duplicating those done previously can be conducted.

Electrophysiologists trace the flow paths through neural networks and examine neural signals to find what transformations have been accomplished by these networks. Physiologists use extirpation to establish the function of various anatomical structures by selectively destroying them. Thus we find electrophysiologists concerning themselves with correlations and time relations between acoustic stimuli and the resulting signals which appear in various parts of the nervous system. Those using extirpation clinical studies interest themselves in the performance of impaired ears and auditory systems. It goes without saying that what the auditory theorists learn from such studies must be reconciled with what they know from psychoacoustics. *What we hear* must be compatible with *how we hear*.

Pulses in the auditory nerve measured by electrophysiologists show fairly definite patterns. If the ear is stimulated by a single tone, the hair cells and neurons in the vicinity of maximum displacement on the basilar membrane are excited. The neurons close to the maximum fire most often; those farther away less often, in accordance with the intensity-frequency behavior. Actually, there is a sequence of events: The traveling wave starts along the cochlear partition from the oval window, increasing in amplitude as it moves. For a tone of moderate intensity, many of the nerves are triggered into action in turn as the wave grows. Beyond the place where the wave reaches its maximum amplitude very few nerves are excited. The cutoff of nerve firings is apparently sharper than the decline in vibration amplitude, indicating some sort of spatial neural inhibition, reminiscent of Békésy's experiments on the skin of the arm. Thus, for low frequencies, nerves over a broader span are excited. This behavior is, of course, in accord with the observed masking of high tones by low tones.

Observations show that the neurons leading from the frequency-selective basilar membrane maintain their identity in the auditory nerve. Their endings in the cochlear nucleus are again separated spatially. Thus we might think of the basilar membrane as being mapped or "unrolled" in the nucleus. In fact, no fewer than thirteen such orderly projections have been

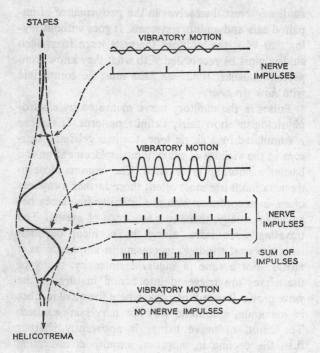

STAPES

VIBRATORY MOTION

NERVE IMPULSES

VIBRATORY MOTION

NERVE IMPULSES

SUM OF IMPULSES

VIBRATORY MOTION
NO NERVE IMPULSES

HELICOTREMA

Fig. 6.5

found in this area alone. Other similar projections have been found as high as the cerebral cortex as well as at in-between stations. Apparently the auditory sense makes capital of the frequency analysis performed in the inner ear.

Physiologists have found that partial destruction of the cochlea tends to raise the threshold of hearing for the frequencies whose place occurs in the destroyed region. Low-frequency tones, however, remain audible if only the part near the oval window, or high-frequency, end of the cochlea is intact. This fact supports the view that perception of low-frequency tones does not depend upon the place of excitation only.

Indeed, for pure tones below about 1500 cps, the nerve impulses carry direct evidence of the pitch. A fixed point on the basilar membrane vibrates at the same rate as the stimulus tone. The maximum of its vibration corresponds to the arrival of the traveling wave at that point. Neurons there tend to fire on this peak, as illustrated in Fig. 6.5.

How Neurons Relay the Message

Generally they do not fire on every peak. As the intensity of the tone is raised, the neurons fire more nearly on every peak. In addition, other neurons with higher threshold begin to fire. If we looked at the totality of pulses carried by the auditory nerve, they would appear as volleys or groups of nerve pulses separated in time by the period of the stimulating tone. That is, the number of volleys per second would be the same as the stimulus frequency. At frequencies greater than perhaps 300 cycles per second a single neuron cannot fire on every peak because of its "dead" period. A bundle of neurons could maintain synchrony by successive firings, and furthermore, such a bundle could produce volleys by the same co-operative process.

This sort of thinking has led to the *volley theory* of pitch perception, as opposed to the place theory. In the volley theory, it is assumed that while intensity may correspond to the average rate of the pulses, pitch is associated with their grouping in time. The place theory also allows a correlation between rate and intensity, but it associates pitch with the position in the cochlea from which the neuron comes, and it disregards the periodic variation in the pulse rate caused by the production of the pulses in successive volleys corresponding in time to the peaks of the sound wave.

Fortunately, we do not have to choose between these theories. The history of science provides many instances in which two or even more theories or models have been necessary to account for the behavior of complicated mechanisms, and with deeper understanding it has been found that both theories were valid, one being applicable in certain circumstances and the second in others. It would not be unusual to find a great deal of flexibility in our sense of hearing. The brain may have several methods for discrimination open to it and at any instant use the one or ones most appropriate to the task at hand.

According to the volley theory, what is sent off to the brain is a sequence of electrical impulses traveling along the neurons which constitute a nerve. The impulses together form a somewhat distorted reproduction of the vibratory motion of the basilar membrane. The reproduction will presumably be best for low-frequency sounds since a group of neurons can supply several pulses during each cycle, and will be poorest for very high frequencies for which an individual neuron can at best supply a pulse only every several cycles.

No matter how good the reproduction is, however, the quality of pitch can only be inherent in it; the pitch of the train of nervous impulses must be derived in some way by the nervous system or by the brain.

We can think of several appropriate mechanisms, but none has a firm basis in physiology. The simplest is merely a device that makes a running count of the volleys and computes their average number. Some theorists think in terms of a "cerebral observer" or leprechaun who "perceives" the simplified information presented by the ear and lower nervous system. This notion arises because it seems strange to us to equate our personal perceptions with impersonal physical events.

Synchronized volleys in the auditory nerve are quite prominent for sine waves below 1000 cps. Above 2000 cps the nerve pulses seem to appear in rather random order; perhaps we use the place principle to discriminate pitch for these higher-frequency sine waves, reserving the volley principle for the lower ones.

We should note, however, that when a sine wave of, for example, 3000 cps is turned off and on periodically, say 100 times per second, prominent volleys at the 100 cps rate are observed. These volleys are synchronized with the *envelope* or outline of the wave. Listening to such a wave, we hear a pitch of 100 cps. This is the same as Schouten's residue phenomenon, in which we hear the fundamental pitch while listening to only its higher overtones. Perhaps the volley principle works at the higher frequencies for complex waves only—waves other than pure sine tones.

It is also possible that for sound whose repetition frequency—that is, fundamental frequency or envelope frequency—is low enough to produce distinct volleys, the place mechanism of the ear is used primarily in judging the timbre or quality of the sound, while some counting or time-comparison operation performed on the volleys is used in judging pitch. (If this is so, a pure tone or sine wave is a very peculiar case and could lead to confusing experimental results, because for a sine wave place and repetition frequency are inseparably tied together.) Such an association of place with timbre and of time-between-volleys with pitch might help to reconcile two conflicting notions of pitch. One arises from the mel scale of pitch for sine waves. The subjectively equal pitch differences of the mel scale are very different from the "equal" differences between musical intervals such as semitones and octaves. Perhaps one should associate the mel scale with a place mechanism and the harmonies of music with a time mechanism.

The notion of synchronized nerve volleys is very useful in explaining binaural interactions. Suppose that each ear received the same pressure wave, but one received it a little later in time than the other. Suppose, further, that after the cochlear filtering action each wave were represented in the nervous system by a series of volleys in time. The volleys from one ear would occur before the corresponding ones from the other. If the nervous system could in some way measure this time disparity, it would have the information we know to be important in binaural hearing.

Perhaps the prettiest neural circuit proposed by the theorists for the purpose of time comparison is shown in Fig. 6.6. Neurons carrying volleys from the two ears lie parallel to each other with their directions of propagation oppositely oriented. Neighboring synapses in each neuron chain are cross-connected to common neuron cell bodies, which require a coin-

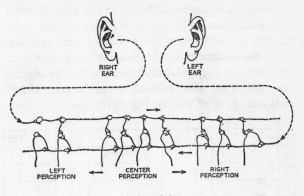

RIGHT
EAR

LEFT
EAR

LEFT
PERCEPTION

CENTER
PERCEPTION

RIGHT
PERCEPTION

Fig. 6.6

cidence of nerve impulses from both neuron chains to fire them. Thus, if the volleys are time-coincident when they enter their respective neuron chains, they will coincide again at the center of the network and will set off the central neuron. If one of the volley trains is delayed, the coincidence point moves toward that side. Thus inter-aural time difference could be mapped into a place co-ordinate and thereby measured.

We saw in Chapter IV that binaural interaction is sensitive not only to time difference between the ears but also to the difference in amplitude or intensity. We tend to localize the source of sound toward the more intense ear or side. The auditory model just outlined can account for this effect also. We need assume merely that volleys in the transmission path leading to the neuron chains from the ears travel faster the higher the intensity of the corresponding stimulus. Thus we can explain the balancing of a time delay at one ear by increased intensity in the same

163

ear to give a center perception (see Fig. 4.9). A series of measurements like that of Fig. 4.9 enables us to deduce how the neural delay changes with intensity. This curve, shown in Fig. 6.7a, is quite similar to the shape of a typical delay curve electrophysiologists have found for volley travel between the ear and medial geniculate of the cat, Fig. 6.7b.

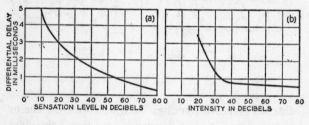

Fig. 6.7

We should not conclude rashly from these remarks that there is in fact such a mechanism in the auditory tract, or even that this particular function is performed in some other way. No one has found a coincident-detecting anatomical arrangement or measured corresponding nerve impulses. Yet it seems worth while to speculate about what mechanisms and operations *could* exist within the framework of present knowledge, for it is only by manipulating ideas that the full significance of new facts can be appreciated and new thoughts evolve.

The attraction of any model is that it tends to bring a number of loosely connected phenomena into a logical relation. For instance, if a pure tone, or sine wave, of frequency f is delayed by a time $\frac{1}{2}f$, it is thereby turned upside down—that is, made the negative of itself. Imagine that we listen to a noise reaching both ears simultaneously, as it might from a source dead ahead, together with a low-frequency tone reaching one ear direct and the other ear inverted (delayed by a time $\frac{1}{2}f$), as it might from a source to one side. In such circumstances we can hear a tone that is around 10 db weaker than if it reached both ears in the same manner, uninverted, undelayed. This seems natural in our model, for it tends to separate the "noise volleys" from the "sine-wave volleys." This is another way of saying that we are using our power of directional discrimination in separating the tone from the noise.

At this point the following phenomenon may or may not surprise us. Suppose we listen to a noise and a tone, both undelayed, with both ears (through two earphones). Suppose we make the noise a few decibels stronger than needed just to mask the tone. Then suppose we turn off the tone in one receiver: while undelayed noise continues to reach both ears, the tone reaches one ear only. We hear the tone clearly, although we could not hear it when it reached both ears! Analysis shows that this is equivalent to hearing a noise source dead ahead and two tone sources, one dead ahead, which is masked by the noise, and one to the side, which is not masked.

Unexplored Territory of the Brain

The models we have discussed—those concerning loudness, pitch, binaural interaction, and masking—hardly do justice to man's massive auditory apparatus. Indeed there is evidence that not all our complex hearing mechanism is necessary for the simpler perceptions. Psychological conditioning experiments have shown that some of the lower forms of animal life, birds and fish for example, are not significantly inferior to man in discriminating tones or localizing sources of sound. Yet their hearing apparatus is much simpler. Fish have neither basilar membrane nor cochlea. The neural equipment of both fish and birds is smaller and lacks the refinement found in man and other mammals. But, as we have seen in Chapter V, we really are not too sure that fish do in fact hear tones; they may perceive them as pressures.

If the mechanisms of pitch perception and binaural localization are similar at various levels on the phylogenetic (pertaining to an animal's *race* history, rather than its *individual* history) scale, then the corresponding operations must be simple indeed and must involve only a modest proportion of man's auditory apparatus.

Another piece of evidence arises out of experience with a disease of the inner ear, Ménière's disease, which is accompanied by spontaneous and disturbing noises in the ear. The auditory nerve is often partially cut to relieve the symptom. Nearly half of the nerve can be sectioned before any impairment of simple tonal response is detected. Significantly, though, the understanding of speech suffers after such an operation. Perhaps only relatively few neurons are required for hearing simple tones while many more are needed for representing the complex aspects of speech.

Indeed, man and mammals can accomplish a far greater variety of auditory tasks of greater complexity than the lower forms can. Our complicated percepts involve recognition of patterns of events in addition to the events themselves. Speech can be viewed as a complex frequency-time-intensity pattern. As Paget found, we can listen to its elementary parts or to its entirety. One's ability to perform both the resolution of subtle attributes of a complex sound and the fusion of independent events into a whole is a matter of learning and volition. It was only after concentrating his attention and training his auditory sense that Paget was able to analyze vowel sounds by ear. Even the simpler ability to discriminate pitch seems to be subject to these factors. Perhaps man's auditory tract must be extensive enough to accommodate both his whims and his ambitions.

Some hint of how we concentrate our attention in audition has been found in experiments with cats. When clicks are produced near the ear of an anesthetized cat, nerve pulses can be observed in the ascending nerve paths and on the auditory regions of the cortex. Dr. Paul Hernandez Peón, now professor of physiology at the University of Concepción in Chile, found the same pulses when he performed the experiment with an unanesthetized animal. However, when a fish was held near the cat's nose, the pulses disappeared. Apparently the cat was concerned with the fish, not with the clicks, and in some way turned off or diverted for another use the nerve paths which had been used to convey the clicks to the brain.

Dr. Robert Galambos, one of the pioneers in auditory electrophysiology, who is now working at Walter Reed Army Medical Center in Washington, found a similar result using caged cats with implanted electrodes which monitored various auditory centers. When clicks were presented to the animals continuously over a period of several days, they no longer "listened" to them, as evidenced by the absence of correlated neural pulses on the electrodes. When

Galambos then applied unpleasant electrical shocks across the cats' chests in synchrony with the clicks, the cats began to take active notice by arching their backs and hissing. After the shocks were discontinued the animals remained disquieted, listening attentively to the clicks. Now there were strong correlated nerve impulses measured at the implanted electrodes.

How these neural impulses are turned off and on at will we do not know. It seems logical, though, that the process may have something to do with those nerve pathways that descend from higher to lower auditory centers. Perhaps higher "control" centers in the brain send down signals which partially squelch the incoming pulses. The control centers in this model receive through the ascending paths only a modest amount of neural data on which they can base their control function, leaving the ascending tract relatively free to "listen" to other sounds. This kind of feedback control is not strange to the nervous system. We have in fact noted in Chapter V that certain little muscles in the middle ear are operated in response to loud sounds so as to reduce the transmission to the inner ear and thus protect it from very loud sounds.

In remarking on the versatility of the auditory tract, we must note its remarkable adaptive powers. For instance, even after much of a cat's auditory cortex is removed it can still differentiate a high-low-high succession of tones from the pattern low-high-low. Only after an extensive removal of the auditory cortex, including some neighboring areas on both sides of the brain, is this ability lost beyond training. Most small cortical lesions have remarkably little apparent effect on such functions.

Indeed, an eminent auditory theorist and psychologist, J. C. R. Licklider of Bolt, Beranek and Newman, Inc., Cambridge, Massachusetts, has stated that one of the basic facts of neurophysiology is that the nervous system works despite a considerable amount of misarrangement of detail. He calls this "the principle of sloppy workmanship." This implies that neural circuits are versatile enough to work despite unreliability of their parts. Thus we might consider the auditory mechanism as, in Licklider's words, "the product of a superb architect and a sloppy workman."

In recent years engineers have begun to learn how to design apparatus with a similar property. The motivation was provided by today's very large electronic machines, which typically contain millions of separate components. Even if each component malfunctioned only once in every million operations, the machine as a whole would scarcely ever work. Often it is not feasible to increase the reliability of the components. The question then arises, how can reliable machines be built out of unreliable components? It seems clear that by duplicating its internal functions often enough the fallibility of a machine's components could be overcome. John von Neumann, the famous mathematician, wrote a paper in the early 1950s describing a method by which this might be done. Claude Shannon of the Massachusetts Institute of Technology and E. F. Moore of Bell Laboratories refined this concept, and recently I have seen a simple machine in which any basic component, such as a wire, fuse, or battery, can be disconnected or short-circuited without altering its operation.

Science is making progress in understanding audition. Perhaps the reader is wondering how far we may eventually go in reducing human processes to physical terms. It may be that science will disclose how we hear, how we feel, how we taste, how we see, how we think, and what motivates us. What will be the result when the gulf between physics and biology is closed, if it can ever be closed? The answers to these questions lie in the distant future, but their philosophical and practical implications have increasing influence on thinking in medicine, psychiatry, the social sciences, economics, and politics. We can hope, at least, that as man learns more about man the human race will find a road somewhere between outright anarchy and the grim sterility of Aldous Huxley's *Brave New World*.

CHAPTER VII

Voices

A few summers ago, a friend told me rather excitedly that he had talked to fish. Since I know several people named Fish, it took a little while to grasp that he had talked to some inhabitants of the Atlantic Ocean off Woods Hole, Massachusetts. They were common sea robins, and it turned out that my friend used the word "talk" rather loosely. Quite in the same fashion as the cricket men of Chapter IV, he had constructed an electronic sea robin, but, since he had first analyzed the sound of the real animal very carefully, he was successful in his attempts to "converse" with these fish. Sea robins produce either a "grunt" or a rattling sound, which my friend (Dr. J. M. Moulton of Bowdoin College, Brunswick, Maine) named a "staccato call." When he produced an artificial staccato call, Moulton was able to get the fish to answer. He went on to tell me in detail how he did it, and how he could suppress the calling of these fish with pure tones between 200 and 600 cycles per second. When I asked him what sea robins used those noises for, and why they should lapse into insulted silence when he played tones for them, he confessed ignorance. "I think," he said, "that the grunts are part of a general alarm reaction, and that the staccato call has to do with breeding and mating behavior. Perhaps the staccato call also serves as a species-recognition device in muddy water; but their shutting up when I play tones to them—that's beyond me." I remarked that it was too bad that he had not been able to see these fish in the murky waters off Woods Hole, and that it would have been so much nicer if he had done his work in the clear tropical waters of the Bahamas or some such place. The twinkle in his eye should have told me—the last time I heard from him he was on his way to Bermuda.

Not too long ago people used to think that the ocean was really the quietest place on earth; "the silent sea" was a cliché everybody believed in. Since the world wars, however, when the military became interested in listening to submarines, that idea has been damaged considerably. The sea may not be the noisiest place in the world, but it is far from silent. All sorts of animals make grunts, whistles, cracks, rattles, and pops. A particular species of shrimp, appropriately called snapping shrimp, closes its claws with a rapid snap that emits a noise loud enough to trip sonic submarine detectors. Indeed, the shrimp used to cause full-blown alarms at many of our coastal defense installations.

Sound Pictures of Sea Robins and Humans

Most of the sounds that can be picked up in the ocean are of unknown origin—that is, we do not know what animal makes which noise. That they are of biological origin, nobody doubts. A striking thing about these sounds is that by and large they are rather simple sounds. By this I do not mean that they are sine waves—far from it; acoustically they are very complex, containing many frequencies. By "simple" I mean to indicate that the pattern of the sounds is simple. For instance, in Fig. 7.1 are shown a simple pattern and a complex pattern. Whether you wish to interpret these patterns as just line patterns or (after defining appropriate co-ordinates) as sound, light, or

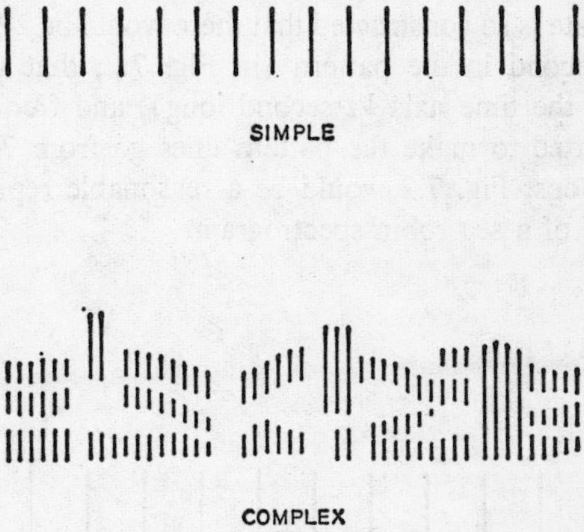

SIMPLE

COMPLEX

Fig. 7.1

touch patterns, makes no difference. It matters not whether the line symbols represent things which are by themselves simple or complex (as defined by another set of measures—in the case of sound, for example, the number of component sine waves); patterns have properties of simplicity or complexity quite independent of the things that make up the patterns. Patterns are not necessarily repetitive, as in our "simple" example, or in wallpaper; the "complex" pattern of Fig. 7.1, for example, is not repetitive.

In sound we may call a series of clicks, such as a clock emits, a simple pattern, but the sound pattern of a symphony orchestra playing Stravinsky's music is utterly complex.

The staccato call of the sea robin is the acoustic equivalent of the simple pattern of Fig. 7.1. Assign appropriate co-ordinates—time and frequency, say—to the pattern, as shown in Fig. 7.2, and you have a *spectrogram* (Chapter III). When the time co-ordinate is so constructed that there would be 22 lines per second in the pattern (in Fig. 7.2, that would make the time axis ½ second long), and frequency is plotted to make the pattern lines go from 700 to 2000 cps, Fig. 7.2 would be a reasonable representation of a sea robin spectrogram.

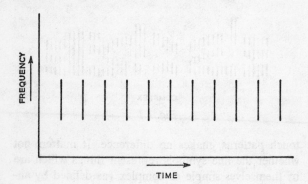

Fig. 7.2

Frogs and toads make sounds that are almost as simple as those of the sea robin. Fig. 7.3 (see Plates) shows a spectrogram of *Xenopus,* a South African toad that lives under water and croaks under water too. You can see that the pattern is just a little more complex than that of the sea robin; the vertical lines consist of two dark parts, and the repetition frequency (number of lines per second) is a good deal higher (about 50 per second). It does, indeed, sound like a croak, while the sea robin sounds like a rattle.

Let us now go from the simple to the complex. Fig. 7.4 (see Plates) shows a spectrogram of human speech; the utterance is: "Speech we may see." Below it you see the conventional English transcription, and a *phonetic transcription,* which we will discuss shortly. Human speech is a very complex pattern: The vertical lines are still closer together, which means the repetition frequency is higher (about 100 per second); the lines consist of several dark sections which can be spaced in different ways and change position. There are open spaces where no sound seems to be present, and there are places where the line pattern changes to a blurry smear. You could call those smears noise. In fact, the sounds they represent, *ch* in *speech* and *s* in *speech* and *see,* are noises that resemble gaussian noise (Chapter III). If you look closely, you can see that the spectrogram consists of successive patterns, which correspond roughly to the sounds we associate with each written letter. The kind of writing we find in a great number of languages is indeed more or less *phonetic.* This means it represents sounds, as opposed to the ideographic way of writing such as is found in Chinese, for instance, where each symbol stands for an *object* or an *idea,* not a sound. But in many languages, and especially English, spelling is no longer (if it ever was) truly representative of the sounds of the language. Just think how many sounds are represented by the conventional spelling *oo* (roof, door, blood) or how many ways there are to write the sound *f* (four, enough, photograph). One of my colleagues the other day wrote on the blackboard the word *ghoti,* and asked me to pronounce it. After I had dutifully fallen into his trap, he told me it was pronounced fish: *f* as in *enough,* *i* as in *women,* and *sh* as in *action!*

Phoneticians (people who study speech and voice) are quite embarrassed, of course, with such ambiguity, and have had to invent an alphabet of their own, in which every symbol represents a unique sound. This is called a *phonetic alphabet.* In this alphabet the *oo's* in *roof, door* and *blood* are written, respectively: u, o and ʌ; the *e, ee* and *ea* in *we, speech* and *sea* are written: i. All languages can, in principle at least, be transcribed with the *international phonetic alphabet,* which is a world-wide standardized set of symbols. Of course, for some strange languages a great number of auxiliary symbols, such as accents, tonality-signs, click-symbols, and so forth, are needed to represent the acoustical events accurately. Even common dialects of English sometimes require special symbols.

Voice of the Frog

What is it now that produces these noises in the first place? What is the mechanism that makes this host of different patterns? Let us go again from the simple to the complex and start with the sea robins. These animals have inside their bodies a *swim bladder,* a tough sac, filled with air or some other gas. This sac is an *acoustic resonator* of the type we discussed in Chapter III. When such a resonator is hit with a quick tap it will vibrate for a short while (depending on its damping) at its resonant frequency. To do the tapping sea robins have a set of *drumming muscles,* a very apt name, because these muscles drum the swim bladder and thus cause it to vibrate with every stroke. The fish has not much control over the signal produced in this fashion; about all it can do is to drum faster or slower. Apparently the "grunt" is a fast roll, while the "staccato call" is a slower rhythm.

The mechanism of voice production of the frog is not precisely known, but it seems to be something like this: The lungs of the animal are closed off from the throat cavity by a *glottis,* a stiff cartilage with a slit in the center. When the frog takes air into the lung, the swallowing movement he makes forces the slit open and air is pushed from the mouth cavity into the lung (Fig. 7.5). When the frog wants to make

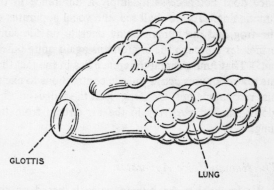

GLOTTIS

LUNG

Fig. 7.5

sound he puts pressure on the lung, the resulting air pressure forces the glottis open for a moment, and a puff of air escapes. The pressure is momentarily equalized and the glottis closes again until the pressure builds up high enough to push another puff of air out. These puffs of air are the taps that excite the frog's resonator, which is his mouth cavity. That cavity is highly stretchable and sometimes even has cheek pouches to produce resonances. The frog has, in principle, a little more control over his voicing than the sea robin has. He can perhaps regulate the repetition rate of the air puffs somewhat (by changing the pressure of the lung on the glottis) and, to some extent, the resonant frequencies (by changing the size or shape of the mouth cavities). Still the frog's abilities in these respects seem to be very limited.

There is a fundamental difference between the voice apparatus of the sea robin and that of the frog as far as the physics of operation is concerned. The anatomical difference is quite obvious, but that difference does not necessarily imply a difference in the functioning. (As we shall see, the vocal apparatus of the frog and the human being operate on the same principles although the anatomy is again quite different.) That fundamental difference lies in the fact that the sea robin uses *active* muscle contractions to excite his resonator, but the frog lets the edges of his glottis-slit flap *passively* in the air stream from the lung.

The Human Voice Apparatus

We know that the human voice is based on the same principle, but before discussing it in some detail, let us look at the anatomy of the vocal organs. Fig. 7.6 shows a diagram of the voice apparatus. The *vocal cords* are equivalent to the edges of the glottis-slit in the frog. They are located in the *larynx,* a cartilaginous box open at the top and the bottom.

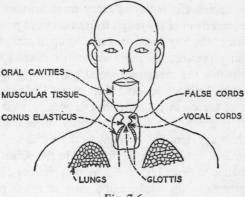

Fig. 7.6

This box appears at the front of the throat as the "Adam's apple." The larynx is the upper end of the respiratory tract; it is the gateway to the lungs. The vocal cords themselves appear from the top as muscle tissue attached to the inner surface of the larynx. Each cord is attached on three sides; thus they are more nearly lips or folds than "cords." The opening between them, again, is called the glottis. Note that the lower surfaces of the cords are formed by a loose membranous covering called the *conus elasticus*. This is attached to the muscular folds only at their edges. We should also note the membranous "false vocal cords," which are superior in position to the vocal cords proper. They probably have no function in normal speech.

The cords are capable of a variety of shapes and motions. In breathing they are held open, providing free access to the lungs. During phonation (production of vocal sound) the cords are brought together by means of an ingenious system of pivoting cartilages

179

and a complex interplay of many small muscles. As air is forced out of the lungs, the same sort of process we saw in the frog (pressure building up, a puff of air escaping, pressure equalized and cords closed again, etc.) makes the cords oscillate at a frequency determined by their tension and their mass. (In men the mass of the cords is larger than in women, and the result is generally a lower frequency of oscillation, which is apparent as lower pitch; the tension of the cords does not seem to be different in the sexes.) It is possible to make high-speed motion pictures of the movements of the cords, and a great deal has been learned from such movies. We must always keep in mind, however, that the movements of the cords determine only the nature of the air puff escaping into the mouth. It is this puff that excites the resonant cavities of the mouth; its shape (fast or slow onset, length, decay time) determines to a large extent the quality of the voice. For instance, a short, sharp pulse of air makes the voice sound crisp and "bright," while a long puff makes it sound mellow and "round." Actors, singers, and other people with trained voices may use these different modes effectively; in ordinary speech, people use a voice varying between these two qualities.

As you see, people have a rather versatile voicing apparatus; they can control pitch by tension of the vocal cords, intensity by the pressure of the lungs, timbre again by the relative tension within the cords (making long or short puffs). A frog apparently cannot do very much with his glottis; it has just a fixed tension and a fixed mass. However, the voice of the frog is not nearly as well understood as the voice of man; when somebody takes a close look at it some day, we may be in for a few surprises.

The versatility of man's voice does not stop at the vocal cords. In fact, an even much greater flexibility for making sounds is provided by the *oral* (mouth) and *nasal* (nose) *cavities,* which are filled with air and form the acoustic resonators that "shape" the air puffs from the glottis into speech sounds. Fig. 7.7 shows the chief features of the complex of organs that

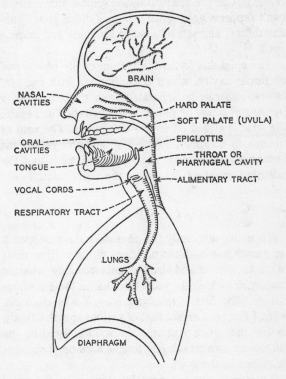

Fig. 7.7

make up the *vocal tract.* The lowermost organ in the tract is the *larynx,* which we have just discussed; beneath it is the *trachea* or windpipe, branching out into the lungs. At the top of the larynx we find the *epiglottis;* it is a "lid" that closes the larynx during swallowing and prevents food or drink from winding up in your lungs instead of your stomach. If accidentally the closure is incomplete when something goes down your gullet (when somebody says something funny just as you are swallowing some coffee and you can't suppress your laugh), it goes down your "Sunday throat" and sets off a reflex coughing and gasping spell.

The epiglottis forms the bottom of the *pharyngeal* or throat cavity, which is continuous with the oral cavity, and can be separated from the *nasal cavity* by the *soft palate* or *velum.* During swallowing, again, the nose is closed off by the soft palate. The roof of the mouth is formed by the hard and soft palate, the bottom by the tongue. The lips and teeth and the nostrils form the front end of the vocal tract.

Frequencies of the Vocal Tract

To understand fully the physical nature of speech we must know both the positions of the various parts of the vocal tract and also the corresponding resonant frequencies which the vocal tract has in these configurations. The first is relatively easy. I was charmed, when I first read an account of various speech sounds, to find that when I uttered the sounds listed by the author my own mouth and tongue took on the shapes described in the book.

To identify the resonant frequencies of the vocal

tract is not so easy. We hear a speech sound as a whole and not as the sum of its parts. In the same way we may hear a chord as a whole in music. Many early workers in the field of speech heard only one resonance in certain vowels, despite prolonged and intensive study. Paget, whiling away time during an illness, was finally able to detect the two lowest resonances of his vocal tract as he whispered vowel sounds. How far it will amuse a reader to observe the position of his tongue, jaw, and lips in uttering various sounds, or to try to detect the resonant frequencies in the sounds he utters, will depend on his skill and inclination.

In any event, let us imagine at least that the tongue lies flat in the mouth as shown in Fig. 7.7 and that the lips and jaw are moderately open. We can achieve this configuration by uttering a sustained vowel intermediately between the vowels of *head* and *had*. Then the oral cavity formed by the tongue together with the roof of the mouth, the teeth, and lips, the soft palate, the epiglottis, and the larynx approximates an organ pipe open at one end. The resonant frequencies of such a pipe are f_0, $3f_0$, $5f_0$, etc., as indicated in Fig. 3.7.

The actual value of the frequency f_0 is determined essentially by the physical length of the tract, although the amount of "flare"—that is, the departure of the tract shape from a simple cylindrical tube—affects the resonant frequency also. Thus, as the mouth is opened wider, f_0 goes up somewhat. For the average man this frequency is near 500 vibrations or cycles per second; for women and children it is typically 727 and 850 cycles per second, respectively. When tongue constrictions are put into the vocal tract, calculation of the resonant frequencies becomes much more difficult, because the tract cannot be approximated by a straight pipe any more.

In spite of this difference in size of vocal tracts and the corresponding difference in the sounds produced, the phonetic value or color of the same vowel pronounced by different speakers can be recognized or perceived without difficulty by the listener. The key to this process lies in the ratio of the resonant frequencies, which are about the same when different speakers utter the same vowel. Thus vowels are similar to musical chords, which maintain their identity when played in various keys. When a person says different vowels, he excites resonances which can differ both in ratio and in absolute frequency.

Varieties of Vowels

In order to produce the twelve distinct vowel sounds used in what is known as "General American" speech, the vocal tract is formed into appropriate shapes. It is possible to describe these in various alternative terms, but in the most convenient approach we treat the tract as a tube whose shape is determined principally by the amount of lip opening and the position of the tongue. The tongue is used to divide the tract into two sections, one in the forward part between the lips and the tongue *hump,* the other between the hump and the vocal cords. As Fig. 7.8 shows, the hump produces a constriction in the tract which can be moved longitudinally. The degree of constriction, as well as its position, is of importance in determining vowel color. The shapes appropriate to the vowels in *eat* and *lost* are shown in Fig. 7.8.

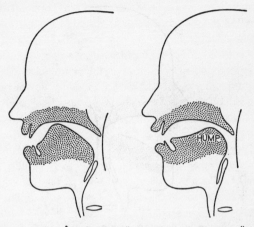

FRONT VOWEL i AS IN "EAT"   BACK VOWEL ɔ AS IN "LOST"

Fig. 7.8

The tongue constriction is in the forward part of the mouth for *eat,* in the rear for *lost,* while the lips are moderately open in both.

It is easy to understand why phoneticians differentiate between the classes of *front* and *back* vowels, referring to the position of the tongue constriction. The effects of degree of tongue constriction can be appreciated by comparing the shape of the tongue for the first vowel in *father,* as shown in Fig. 7.9, with that for *eat.* In the former, there is little tongue constriction. Indeed, the jaw is held more open than in uttering the vowel of *eat.* Thus, in addition to the front-back distinction, the terms *open* and *closed* must be used to describe vowels. Together, these articulatory designations lead to a convenient classification of the vowel sounds, as shown in Table I.

185

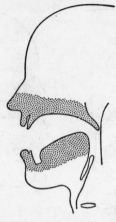

OPEN VOWEL α AS IN "F<u>A</u>THER"

Fig. 7.9

TABLE I

DEGREE OF CONSTRICTION	TONGUE HUMP POSITION		
	Front	Central	Back
CLOSED	i – heed		u – who'd
	ɪ – hid	ɝ – heard	ʊ – hood
MID	e – haid		o – hoed
	ɛ – head	ʌ – hud[1]	ɔ – hawed
OPEN	æ – had		ɑ – hod

Phonetic symbols and key words have been included in Table I. Only vowels used in General American speech have been considered. Positions in which

---

[1] The symbol ə is used to designate the unstressed neutral vowel, called *schwa*, which occurs commonly, for example, as the second vowel in *custom*. The schwa is given an "*r*-coloring" in words such as *moth*ER, in which case it is symbolized by ɝ.

foreign vowels would fall are scattered through the table. In distinguishing these from English vowels, we must introduce the further articulatory distinction of degree of lip-rounding. Lip-rounding is a feature in English vowels also, but since most back vowels are rounded and front vowels unrounded, the description is superfluous. Certain non-English vowels combine rounding with front tongue position. When the vowels are spoken in context some are "held" longer than others. For instance, the vowel in *heed* is longer than that in *hid*. Additional short vowels are *head, hud* and *hood*. The others are generally longer in duration.

The resonant frequencies of tubes of irregular shapes are not harmonics, and further, they are not simply related to the dimensions, as in a uniform pipe. In the sound of *eat* the lowest resonance can be approximately identified with the back or pharyngeal cavity resonating as a closed pipe; the second resonance can be considered as arising in the front or mouth cavity, which resonates as a partially open tube. The third resonance of the tract as a whole may be accounted for as the second resonance of the pharyngeal cavity. For the average male speaker the frequencies are 270, 2290, and 3010 cycles per second. These resonances are commonly called *formant frequencies,* or simply *formants*.

The kind of approximation indulged in here cannot be carried very far. To account for the resonant frequencies it is in most instances necessary to consider the tract as a whole, for the resonant frequencies cannot be identified with the sizes of specific sections. Through studies of vocal tract models and X-ray photographs of speakers' heads and necks, approximate relations between articulator positions and resonance frequencies have been established.

Typical values of vowel formant frequencies for men are given in Table II.

TABLE II

	heed	hid	head	had	hod	hawed	hood	who'd	hud	heard
f_1	270	390	530	660	730	570	440	300	640	490
f_2	2290	1990	1840	1720	1090	840	1020	870	1190	1350
f_3	3010	2550	2480	2410	2440	2410	2240	2240	2390	1690

Classes of Consonants

The consonant sounds are a bit more difficult to describe than the vowels; it would take us too far afield to describe them in detail in a book as modest in size as this. Let us, therefore, have only a brief look at them. We can, again, divide the consonants in various classes, depending on the way they are produced. First, we have a main division into *continuants* and *plosives* (sometimes called *stop consonants*). The continuants are so named, because they can be "held" continuously until you run out of breath. The stop consonants are short and cannot be held. Both classes can be subdivided in *voiced* and *voiceless* sounds, depending on whether the vocal cords are used in their production or not. For instance, *b* is a voiced, *p* is a voiceless, stop consonant. The same goes for the other

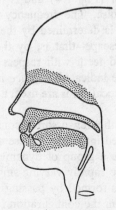

NASAL **m** AS IN "ME"

Fig. 7.10

members of the plosive class: *d–t* and *g–k*. Among the continuants we can again distinguish voiced and voiceless sounds. Exclusively to the voiced group belong the *nasals* (m, n and ŋ, as in si*ng*). They are produced by closing the mouth and dropping down the velum, so that the nasal cavity is connected to the rest of the vocal tract (Fig. 7.10). The air puffs from the glottis excite the nasal as well as the oral cavities (which now resemble a *closed* pipe). The nose cavities have a tortuous shape and a soft lining of mucous membranes. The effect on sound going through them is that the higher harmonics in the voice puffs are damped out, and about all that remains is the lowest resonant frequency. The other continuants are the *fricatives* and they again may be voiced or voiceless. In both, sound is produced in the mouth, by letting air escape through constrictions between lips and teeth. This makes the hissing sound we encountered earlier (Fig. 7.4) and is really something like gaussian noise. The frequency content of the noise, however, is determined by the particular way we let the air escape—that is, by the *placement* of tongue, lips, and teeth with respect to each other. These effects are indicated as *place* in Table III. If, in addition, the vocal cords are used, a voiced fricative is the result.

We are left with a few assorted consonants that we have not yet fitted into any of these classes.

The *glides* are a group of dynamic sounds. They can be likened to rapidly varying single vowels. The r sound in *red* is formed by passing the articulators rapidly away from the configuration for the vowel ɝ, (*heard*). There is the same relation between the glide w (*we*) and the vowel u (*who'd*), and between the

TABLE III

PLACE	VOICING	SOUND
Lip to Teeth	Voiceless	f – *fill*
	Voiced	v – *vest*
Tongue to Teeth	Voiceless	θ – *thick*
	Voiced	ð – *this*
Tongue to Gum Ridge	Voiceless	s – *see*
	Voiced	z – *zoo*
Tongue to Hard Palate	Voiceless	ʃ – *shed*
	Voiced	ʒ – *pleasure*
Glottal	Voiceless	h – *hat*

glide *j* (*you*) and the vowel i (*heed*). Finally, the *l* as in *lateral* is formed by raising the tip of the tongue to contact the roof of the mouth just behind the teeth. The *l* sound is often classified as a *liquid*.

This enumeration of speech sounds shows that the English language has a wealth of resources out of which to build words. Actually, however, the list grossly oversimplifies American speech. The listed sounds and the tongue, lip, jaw, and velum positions associated with them typify classes of sounds rather than distinct sounds typical of speech. When for example, we utter the stop consonant *t* in various words in connection with various vowels and consonants, the position of closure in the mouth may wander startlingly from that described, and so, we presume, must the acoustical event, although we associate all these sounds in our mind with the letter *t*. One astute phonetician has found some ninety possible varieties of *t* in English speech. In one, in which the *t* is wedged between two other stop consonants, as in the sequence *rapt delirium,* no sound at all is produced corresponding to the *t!*

191

The groups of acoustic events that call up the same linguistic element are called *phonemes*. The vowels and consonants listed in the tables and the text of this chapter are the phonemes of the General American dialect. If you care to count them, you will find that there are thirty-five; I have not mentioned a few phonemes, such as the *diphthongs* (combination-vowels), for instance aɪ, as in *hide*. In all, depending somewhat on the particular dialect, English uses about forty phonemes. There are languages which use as many as sixty and some which use only twenty phonemes.

We have seen in Chapter I that voices of man and beast are used not only for communication, but also for finding food and avoiding obstacles. The insect-eating bats are the best known of these "hunters by ear," but there are also aquatic animals that use echolocation. One of the best-investigated ones is the bottle-nosed dolphin or porpoise, of acrobatic fame. These animals can detect such obstacles as poles and bars under water (even very muddy water during an overcast night!). They can hear the presence of a fish, and pursue and catch it by echolocation, just as the bat catches insects. The noises they make sound something like the creak of a rusty door hinge. In fact, they consist (just as the creaking of a hinge) of a series of short pulses of noise, containing frequencies up to at least 100,000 cps. Just how these animals make their sounds is not known. A lot more is known about the sounds of bats, mostly from the remarkable work of Donald R. Griffin, Professor of Zoology at Harvard. Bats produce a very high frequency sound, between 20,000 and 100,000 cps. Some bats emit long steady whistles, concentrated in a narrow beam. They sweep this beam back and forth by movements of the head and thus "scan" the space in front of them, much as you would sweep the beam of a flashlight across a path. Other bats emit very short pulses that are, moreover, *frequency modulated;* such pulses start at a high frequency, say 60 kc (Kilocycles: units of 1000 cycles. In this case, therefore, 60,000 cycles.), and in a millisecond or so come down in frequency to about 30 kc. It is not very difficult to build an "electronic bat" which produces the same sort of signal; in Fig. 7.11 (see Plates) is shown a spectrogram of a series of pulses from such an artificial bat. A whole book could be written about bats and their sonar. Happily, Dr. Griffin has done just that. It appears in the Science Study Series under the title, *Echoes of Bats and Men.*

In this chapter we have barely scratched the surface of the fascinating world of speech, animal sounds, communication, and echo-sounding. I hope that I have given you a glimpse exciting enough to stimulate you to learn more about it. As we acquire a better understanding of speech and the ways people talk to each other, we may, someday, understand what the process of "talking to one's self," or "thinking," really is.

CHAPTER VIII

Quality and Fidelity

In approaching the subject of "high fidelity," or quality, I walk on tip-toe. These words have become esoteric not only to the lay public but to the engineers and scientists as well. They seem to have various meanings for various people, and the uninitiated can find as many interpretations as "experts" in the field. Some of my friends have said that all the fuss over hi-fi is nonsense. You should not listen to hi-fi; you should listen to the music or the voice. There is something to this point of view. It is certainly a perversion to be so concerned with woofers, tweeters, preamplifiers, and the like that the subjective pleasures of listening become secondary.

The music-is-the-thing theme is an extreme view, however—it is a typical reaction against the faddists. When pressed, many of the most die-hard reactionaries will admit that some music reproducers are satisfactory, others not; that some long-distance telephone connections are better than others; that they get more pleasure from presence at a live performance than from listening to a poor recording.

It is certainly true that high fidelity concerns the

auditory values as well as the mechanical and electronic ones. Thus psychoacoustics and the ear-brain should have some relevance. I was amused by a cartoon showing a very old man with a hearing aid bending forward to catch the super-fidelity output from his expensive and massive system. It is senseless to reproduce sound to which the auditory sense is deaf. This is true for us all, if perhaps in a lesser degree than for the cartoon character. Too, it is sensible to attend to those factors which do bear on auditory sensation.

This approach has a certain "face validity" for those of us who prefer logic to intuition. But, lest we expect too much, let us admit at the outset that the sensation experienced in listening to music, or in hearing a well-read bit of poetry or prose or the voice of an absent friend or relative, is a highly personal experience. It may involve communication of the most subtle feelings. Emotion, passion, sentiment, as well as thought, can be projected via that wave motion which we call sound. To expect that such complex experiences can be reduced to physical formulae is naive. Individual reaction covers a wide range—one man's meat may be another's poison. After all that we know is said, we must fall back on the subjective in our judgment. Listening is the true test, and, I may remark, it is a rare "high-fidelity" system that can reproduce a person's voice well enough to fool a listener who has heard the person speak directly a second or so earlier.

The concepts behind popular notions of quality and fidelity are sometimes confused. We know, for instance, that voices have distinctive qualities of their own. Some are hoarse, some are harsh, some are breathy, and some are nasal. *Voice quality* is typical of the person speaking—it is one of the characteristics that help us to identify voices, moods, and emotions. It gives color to speech and contributes to individuality.

Distorted transmission can rob speech of much of its natural quality. As the fidelity of a connection decreases, the reproduced voice becomes less distinctive. Anyone who has heard short-wave communication on a poor night will appreciate that highly distorted speech, while it is still to some degree intelligible, has little of the character or mood of the person speaking. It may appear to the listener that the circuit is superimposing its own qualities upon those of the speaker's voice and thereby displacing or masking them. We may be hard pressed to recognize the speaker or to identify his emotion. If the circuit is poor enough, even intelligibility becomes impaired, and further degradation may render any communication difficult. Hence *transmission quality* or *fidelity,* or *fidelity of reproduction,* is concerned with how faithfully voice naturalness, as well as intelligibility, is preserved. We must be careful to distinguish between voice quality and the quality or fidelity of reproduction. The former concerns the talker, the latter the circuit.

Musical instruments have their typical qualities too. A flute and an oboe, as we saw in Chapter III, sound different even when playing the same note (Fig. 3.10). We say each has a distinctive *timbre* or tone color. Timbre is determined by the relative strengths of an instrument's overtones, which are the harmonics of its fundamental pitch. Needless to say, if these relations are disturbed in transmission the timbre too is altered, an alteration which reflects audibly the shortcomings of the circuit. For instance, if a violin were played inside a barrel, the resonances of the barrel would themselves be excited. The barrel-like timbre would be mixed with that of the violin. An electrical circuit which strongly emphasizes energy at some frequencies and suppresses it at others can act like an electrical barrel, lending something of its own to any signal passed through it. Because musical sound generally contains a much broader range of frequencies and intensities than speech, it is more sensitive to this effect. High-quality reproduction tends to preserve voice quality or musical timbre. If we look through a highly polished piece of glass, the objects on the other side appear real and undistorted. Similarly, we can perceive "sound objects" by listening to their sound through a "transparent" or high-fidelity reproduction system.

Causes of Distortion

High-fidelity reproduction is dependent upon equipment free from faults. After a sound arrives at a microphone pickup, its quality can be impaired by the same distortions that affect speech intelligibility. Bandwidth limitation on both high and low end, non-uniform response to various frequencies within the reproduced band (such as are produced by the barrel), non-linear distortion, and introduction of alien noise can and do result from deficiencies in reproducing apparatus.

A typical connection of components is shown in Fig. 8.1. A pickup (microphone, tape recorder, radio tuner, or phonograph cartridge) provides a low-level, or faint, input signal to a preamplifier which brings the signals to the higher level appropriate for input to a power amplifier. This in turn drives a loudspeaker or sound radiator. The most serious deficiencies reside usually in the pickup or the radiator. Note that these components have both an electrical and a mechanical function: they convert mechanical action to electrical waves or vice versa. Engineers have found that the electromechanical links in a reproducing system are its weakest.

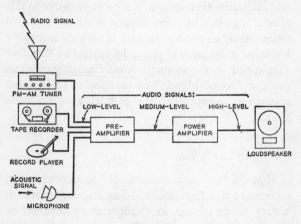

Fig. 8.1

For instance, the intensity of a sine wave tone radiated by an expensive ($150 class) loudspeaker varies quite markedly with the frequency of the tone. If we plot the intensity of the tone expressed in decibels as the frequency is varied over the audio band, we obtain a frequency response curve. (As noted in Chapter III, a valid measurement can be made only in a room whose walls absorb sound almost completely—an echoless or anechoic chamber.) It shows how the

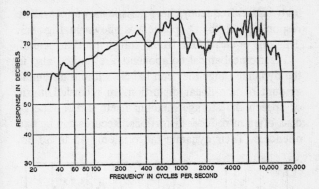

Fig. 8.2

component tones making up speech or music would be altered when reproduced through the speaker. Such a plot for the expensive speaker is shown in Fig. 8.2. Note that the variation between 40 and 14,000 cycles per second is about 10 decibels up and down from the center level. These variations are not abrupt, however, and this speaker would probably superimpose little of its own quality on the reproduced sound. In this sense it is a "good" speaker, however shock-

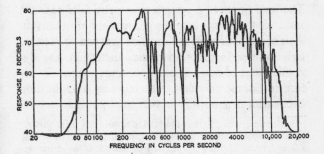

Fig. 8.3

199

ingly bad its frequency characteristic may appear. The response of a "bad" speaker[1] is shown in Fig. 8.3. This one is clearly far from "transparent" to sound.

Electromechanical components are limited also in the dynamic range they can handle without an undue amount of non-linear distortion. In recorded music or speech the storage medium itself, either tape or disc, often introduces distortions. Records can be bad offenders. Their dynamic range is only 45 to 50 db.

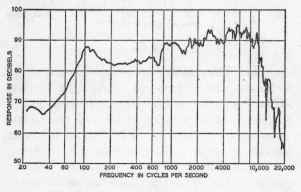

Fig. 8.4

The loud finale of a symphony usually falls near the inside of the disc, where the grooves are most curved. This combination yields distortion that can be particularly severe. In order to reduce distortion, the dynamic range of music is often cut down artificially before recording. In effect, the recording amplification is changed dynamically so that loud passages are re-

[1] It costs about $50, but the reader should not infer that all speakers show such poor responses, or that the curve of Fig. 8.2 is typical of $150 speakers. For instance, the other response curve shown in Fig. 8.4 is beautifully smooth and broad. It came from a speaker costing $19.95.

duced in volume. This procedure permits a broader volume range to be recorded without distortion, but it means, of course, a compression of the normal volume range of recorded material.

In addition to these effects, records and sometimes magnetic tape produce an audible "frying" noise. On records it is known as needle or surface scratch.

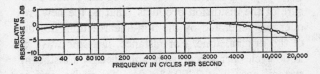

Fig. 8.5

In comparison, amplifiers are relatively free of trouble. Standard units can cover the audible frequency band smoothly and introduce little non-linear distortion. The same statements apply to the average radio tuner. The frequency response of a $45, four-watt power amplifier is shown in Fig. 8.5. Thus amplifiers are less liable to distort the frequency content of signals passing through them. Unless tuners and amplifiers are in good repair and are properly installed, however, they are liable to contribute hissing noise or low-frequency hum.

Annoyance Factor

So much for the sources of these imperfections. Which of them are important to the auditory sense? Non-linear distortion is probably the most annoying. It is audible even in small amounts. It adds a harsh and unnatural sound to music and voice. If you have

201

ever turned up your radio volume full, by accident perhaps, you have probably heard a severe case of non-linear distortion. The speaker may have seemed to blare forth a violently disturbing noise little related to what you heard after reducing the volume.

The amount of distortion in a system is usually specified in percentages. For the radiated sound, this number is equivalent to the ratio of the sound pressure of the distortion products (that is, the new frequencies generated by the non-linear action) to that of the original tone. For instance, if a sine wave of 1000 cycles per second were amplified by a distorting system, energy at 2000, 3000, 4000 cycles, and so on would be generated. A 3 per cent distortion figure would mean that the ratio of the distortion pressure (including energy at all frequencies) to that of the 1000-cycle wave at the amplifier output would be .03. This figure may seem low but it represents only a 30-db differential in intensity. In terms of subjective loudness, a medium-pitched sound can be 30 db weaker than a low-pitched sound and still be louder to our ears.

As in this example, distortion is often measured with a single sine-wave signal, although two are sometimes employed. What does such a figure tell us about the quality when, say, a symphony is reproduced by the apparatus? Directly it tells us little since the "annoyance factor" depends not only upon the nature of the signal, its sound level, and the nature of the non-linear effect, but also upon the listener. Harry F. Olson and his collaborators at the Radio Corporation of America have done much to clear up this question. Even so, their results do not give the whole answer since they used only two systems and a small group of listeners. Nevertheless, their conclusions are a good general guide and show clearly an effect often spoken of loosely in hi-fi circles as "balance" or "matching components."

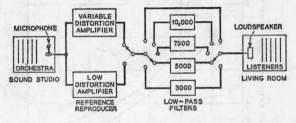

Fig. 8.6

In these experiments Olson used the apparatus shown in Fig. 8.6. The "reference" reproducer, the best equipment available at the time, produced less than 0.3 per cent distortion, and covered 45 to 15,000 cps smoothly. The "distorting" system was identical except that it could be adjusted to produce a range of percentage distortions (measured with sine wave input). In addition, the effective high-frequency cutoff of both systems could be changed in four steps from 15,000 to 3750 cps. Live speech and orchestral music were played through these systems. Listeners were queried to find the setting of the distorting system which was just perceptibly different from the reference system. The percentage sine wave distortion for this setting might then be defined as the limit for hi-fi reproduction. A similar determination was made for the distortion *tolerable* in low-grade ("lo-fi") equipment; and finally the amount which rendered the system definitely *objectionable* was measured. The listeners' judgments were found to depend strongly on the fre-

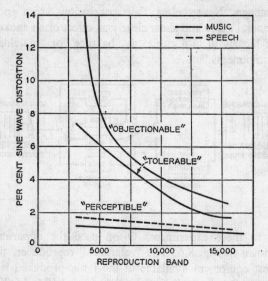

Fig. 8.7

quency band of the system. A summary of the result is shown in Fig. 8.7. Note that speech is less affected by distortion than music. More importantly, the broader the frequency range covered, the lower must be the distortion for good results. For instance, if the upper cutoff is 15,000 cycles per second, 0.7 per cent is permissible, while about twice that amount is still imperceptible when all the energy above 3750 cps is eliminated. Wide-band systems are much more susceptible to distortion than those covering a more restricted band. Wide-frequency coverage is not desirable unless it is accompanied by low distortion.

How Wide the Bandwidth?

A wide-band system is not necessarily hi-fi. For instance, a low-distortion "20 to 20,000 cps" amplifier and loudspeaker combination is actually detrimental if it is preceded in the chain of components by a unit producing distortions greater than those indicated in the preceding figure. It is my opinion, based on experience with many music reproducers, that very few commercially available disc recordings meet this test, particularly after being played a few times (even with an expensive needle). More often than not, the very-high-frequency energy is eliminated by the record manufacturer so that it never reaches the disc. Or the radio studio or listener is forced to reduce the energy level drastically by turning down the treble control, and perhaps by other electrical filtering, to keep the distortion within tolerable bounds.

Most discussions of hi-fi imply that, apart from distortion, broad frequency coverage is desirable for pleasant listening. What could be more logical than striving to reproduce the entire range of frequencies audible in the sound of an orchestra or concert? Unfortunately, preference experiments fail to support this view. Two Columbia Broadcasting System engineers, Howard A. Chinn and Philip Eisenberg, in 1945 tested listeners' preference, using both live and recorded classical music over three systems. The "wide" one responded evenly to energy in the range 40 to 10,000 cps; the "medium" one, 80 to 7000 cps; and the "narrow" one, 180 to 4000 cps. Their subjects preferred the narrow to the wide 58 per cent to 15 per cent (27 per cent had no preference), and the

205

medium to the wide 67 per cent to 12 per cent (21 per cent no preference). These figures led to conclusions disturbing to the hi-fi fraternity and were the subject of heated debate for several years after their publication. Did Chinn's and Eisenberg's equipment produce enough distortion so that they were measuring the same effect that Olson found? I do not know the answer to this question, but certainly these investigators were not novices in the audio equipment field.

More recently Roger E. Kirk of Ohio State University confirmed, at least in part, the Chinn and Eisenberg finding. He used four systems: three were similar to theirs; the fourth covered 30 to 15,000 cps. Again the system of widest range came off at the bottom of the list for practically all material played. Kirk attributes this result to the psychological "set" of the listeners. He says that most people learn to expect a restricted frequency range in music from a loudspeaker. Anything that departs from their expectation sounds strange; people prefer the familiar. To document this view, Kirk separated his subjects into three groups. The first spent sessions listening to the wide-range system over a six-week period. The second listened to the narrow-range system, and the third did no organized listening. On repeating his tests after the six weeks, he found that the first group's preference had shifted toward the wide system, the second group's toward the narrow system, while the third group's preference remained about the same. Thus it would seem frequency-range preference is an acquired taste. If you are a hi-fi addict, the high-tone squeak and low-tone boom add to your listening pleasure—to you wide-range music sounds "crisp" and "mellow." If you are not yet initiated, you may have to work hard to acquire the expensive taste for wide-band reproduction.

Does Chinn's and Eisenberg's result mean that Mr. Average Listener would be better pleased if in the concert hall too the lows and highs were somehow removed before the sound reached his ears? The answer is no! There is a vast difference between listening in the concert hall to a live performance and listening in the living room to a loudspeaker. In the latter it is as though the listener were hearing the concert through a hole the size of his loudspeaker. The effect could be almost duplicated if the listener's room were transported bodily to the concert hall and his speaker replaced by a mere porthole through which the sound entered his room. The porthole should be positioned in the hall to coincide with the particular microphone location used for recording or radio pickup. We have in this model replaced all the electronic and electro-mechanical gear intervening between the orchestra and the listener with an acoustic connection. The model shows how the acoustical properties of the hall and the listening room, as well as microphone placement, are factors in the quality of reproduced music. Indeed, we have no difficulty in hearing the reverberation characteristics of the recording studio or hall in listening to a reproduced performance. But we also realize that we are hearing it in a highly artificial way —that is, through a small opening in our living room.

In this situation, too, the listener has lost all sense of auditory perspective. He cannot tell that the violins are here, the cellos over there, and the soloist in the middle. He cannot appreciate that the music has a spatial as well as a tonal dimension. To him, all the sound comes from one location—his loudspeaker.

Olson showed, in an ingenious experiment, that these factors exert a major influence in determining listeners' frequency-range preference. He used an orchestra sitting behind a visual screen as his sound source. His subjects, however, had no way of knowing whether the music was live or reproduced. The frequency content of the sound reaching the listeners was changed by means of a "vertical venetian blind" between the orchestra and the visual screen. When open, the blind allowed the full range of audible frequencies to pass; when closed, it removed the energy above 5000 cps, much as a door or thin wall would. Thus it acted as an acoustical filter serving the same function as Chinn's and Eisenberg's electrical filters. There was no chance for non-linear distortion or the "hole-in-the-living room" effect to creep in. Alternating between the two conditions, Olson found a 2-to-1 preference for wide-range music, and a 3-to-1 preference for wide-range speech.

Binaural and Stereophonic Systems

If what one really wants to do is bring the concert or talker to the listener in a remote place, then auditory "perspective" must be created there. At present two methods are known whereby this can be accomplished: these are *binaural* and *stereophonic* reproduction. Both are based upon the use of more than one pickup or microphone.

By a binaural system we mean a system in which a distinct, separate sound path is provided to each ear. To accomplish this, two microphones are placed in an artificial "head" so that one picks up the sound that would be heard by a person's right ear, while the other serves as a left ear. These two signals are amplified and transmitted separately and are fed to the ears of the remote listener by separate headphones. The effect thus created is very compelling; acoustically his ears have been transported to the scene of activity. Auditory perspective abounds; it is said that listeners pull in their feet instinctively when a person walks in front of the dummy. Furthermore, the ability to concentrate on sound from a particular direction is recreated. This, together with the ability mentally to "squelch" unwanted sound in the environment, indicates how effective the illusion can be. It is altogether different from listening to a single channel with both ears.

The binaural system as we have described it, suffers from one defect. When the listener rotates his head, the acoustical world rotates with him rather than remaining fixed. He is always facing the orchestra no matter which way he turns. Moreover, while the listener has a sense of right and left in relation to a sound source, it does not seem external to him but rather inside his head or near his ear. This deficiency can be remedied by providing an electrical link which turns the dummy's head to match the head motions of the listener.

As we saw in Chapter IV, the cues for binaural localization are time-of-arrival and intensity differences at the two ears. Note, however, that the same differences can be produced by sources in front and behind the listener as indicated in Fig. 8.8. There is, then, a phantom source in addition to the true one. This diagram shows also how we ordinarily resolve the front-

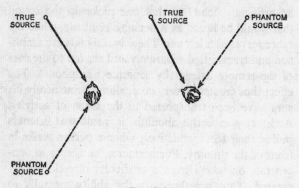

Fig. 8.8

back ambiguity by turning our heads. Thus the rotation link in the binaural system serves an important function.

As convincing as the binaural system is, it requires the use of a headset, itself an artificiality. When loudspeakers are used, auditory perspective is more difficult to sham, but it can be approximated in stereophonic reproduction. Consider the sound wave traveling across stage footlights on its way from source to listener. If we placed many microphones in a curtain above the footlights and connected them to many corresponding loudspeakers above the footlights in a distant hall, the sound wave could be reproduced. A listener's ears would receive the same acoustic wave in either place and auditory perspective would be preserved. But what is the minimum number of microphone-loudspeaker pairs which need be used to produce a convincing effect? To differentiate right from left only, and not the up-and-down dimension, three pairs are sufficient. Even two give an astonishingly lifelike effect.

Of course, just two sources cannot precisely duplicate a sound wave for an audience. The human auditory perceptual mechanism evidently likes to be fooled, and it provides by no means inconsiderable help in creating the illusion. While the exact mechanism is not understood, the precedence effect probably comes into play strongly. Fig. 8.9 illustrates a situation equivalent to a two-channel stereophonic system. Here windows replace the microphone-loudspeaker pairs on an otherwise sound-opaque wall. A

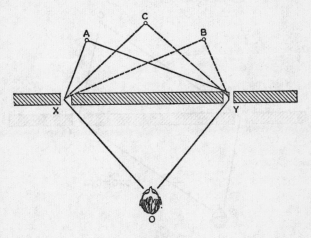

Fig. 8.9

violin at point *A* produces two sound waves at the listener's ears, one traveling the path *AXO,* the other *AYO.* Note that the former path is shorter than the latter and that the sound wave from *X* arrives at the listener before that from *Y.* Consequently he will tend to locate the violin near speaker *X,* a position coinciding roughly with its true position. The opposite state of affairs obtains with a source at point *B*. If a source is near the center, such as at point *C*, the two waves will arrive about simultaneously and result in a "center" perception. Note that when the listener moves off the center line between the speakers the precedence effect still gives him a sense of perspective, but the perceived "stage" is distorted. For instance, "center" as defined by equal travel time is moved to the right when the observer moves to the left (see Fig. 8.10).

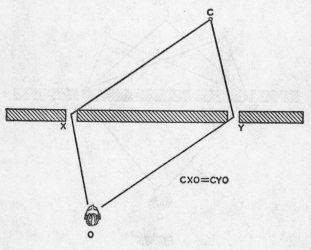

$$CXO = CYO$$

Fig. 8.10

But distortions of this kind are not very serious. The stereo effect is principally a separation in space of the various sound sources. The correct positioning of the sources is not usually important for the listener. The mere fact that the instruments of an orchestra, for instance, are spread out is sufficient to avoid the "muddled" or "blurred" sound typical of single-channel reproduction.

Indeed, many different arrangements of microphones and loudspeakers have been proposed to produce stereophonic effects. One of the most successful has been the use of binaurally placed microphones with widely spaced loudspeakers. There are even methods for producing pseudo-stereo sound from single-channel signals. For instance, if we listen to a single-microphone output reproduced from two separated loudspeakers, we find that music so heard has more "body" and "fullness" than when heard from one alone. The effect is heightened by moving closer to one speaker than the other or by delaying the music signal 20 to 40 milliseconds before feeding it to one of the speakers. While this arrangement does not achieve a true separation of the instruments, the "hole-in-the-wall" sensation is relieved.

Stereo sound is used with many of the new large-screen motion picture presentations. I find that I derive some additional pleasure from the perspective thus created. My wife, on the other hand, finds it disturbing; she is accustomed to "flat" sound in motion pictures. Stereophony is not a cure-all for sound projection. Still, studies have shown equal preference among listeners between 5000-cps-range stereophonic and 15,000-cps-range single-channel systems. Olson repeated his "venetian blind" test using stereo-reproduced sound and found that broad-band coverage is preferred here just as in the case of a live performance, in contrast to single-channel reproduction.

What the reader will prefer I do not know. One thing is certain, however: the New York Philharmonic or the Boston Symphony cannot be transferred perceptually to the living room. There will always be some disparity between the experiences and sensations of the concert hall and those of home listening.

Using stereophonic reproduction in a concert hall, how convincing can the "presence" illusion be made? R. Vermeulen of the Philips Research Laboratory in Holland did an experiment to find out. He had listeners compare the same pieces of music reproduced stereophonically and played live behind a thin but opaque curtain. The tests took place in an auditorium, and the listeners were asked to differentiate between the two presentations. After a statistical analysis of the results he concluded that on the average his subjects could hear the difference only half the time. Those people who could differentiate consistently were in the minority, a mere 16 per cent of the subjects. Tests of this kind demonstrate that in the right environment sound equipment can be almost perfect if enough care is taken and enough money is spent.

To most of us who are interested in high fidelity, this conclusion is perhaps interesting but beside the main point. We have no concert hall in which to reproduce music. Most of the recordings and radio outlets to which we have access are neither stereophonic nor binaural, but single channels of limited fidelity. Furthermore there is the pocketbook to consider. Within such limitations, how can we realize the greatest pleasure? This is a question the individual will have to resolve for himself. After he makes peace with his auditory sense, who is to say that he is wrong?

The difficulties encountered in the reproduction of sounds, and especially of orchestral music, are eloquent testimony to the sensitivity and discrimination of our sense of hearing. It is very hard indeed to try to fool the auditory sense; you may not be able to put your finger on just *what* it is that does not sound right, but you know live music from recorded music just as you know a movie from a real-life scene.

Yet this does not detract from our wonder and awe that so small a set of organs as the human ear and brain, taking up just a few cubic inches of space inside the head, is endowed with powers of discrimination that our best and bulkiest instruments are barely able to match. True, we have instruments that are more sensitive than the ear in some respects, but to try to build a single instrument with such a range and resolution in so small a space is more than any present-day engineer (and, I am sure, engineers for a long time to come) would care to tackle.

CHAPTER IX

The Past Is Prologue

In a Dutch high school there is an excellent biology teacher who teaches the difficult subject of genetics so well that even on the college and graduate level his students never have had to work very hard to pass their genetics courses. What is remembered most about Dr. Meijknecht, though, is the way he gets across to his students the fundamental fact that science is never static, but is ever moving and changing, constantly being rebuilt, expanded, and refined. On occasion his students pointed out to him that what he told them was in conflict with the textbook (a work dating from remote antiquity, in its umpteenth unrevised edition). He then sternly peered over his glasses and announced emphatically, *"I am the book."*

Any book written about a scientific subject is doomed to become obsolete sooner or later. The more active the work which goes on in a field, the quicker do the ideas, theories, and even "facts" in that field become obsolete. This is inevitable; a more precise measurement, a new technique for expressing and manipulating complex relationships, a previously neglected discrepancy between two sets of measurements

216

—all lead to correction, amplification, and adjustment in knowledge. Unfortunately, popular accounts and newspaper articles are apt to use sensational terms, depicting such refinements as an overthrow of well-established knowledge. Some of what is known today is reasonably certain, much more is uncertain, and a very large portion is only dimly understood. It is largely in this third area that basic research is carried out; the first category, the reasonably certain one, constitutes what is usually found in textbooks. Yet often, as a result of basic research, the textbook must be modified.

In this book we have tried to give you a glimpse of what is known about hearing and voice production. While part of it presents reasonably certain knowledge, we have not hesitated to take you into uncertain territory and even into the realm of speculation. Perhaps this small volume can give you some feeling of the active struggle for understanding which goes on in laboratories throughout the world. It is like watching baseball, football, or any other form of competition; if you have played it yourself, however clumsily and poorly, you will understand its true excitement. No amount of book learning of the rules of the game will ever give you more than a sort of aesthetic appreciation—the very soul of the game will be lost to you. While almost every one of us played football, baseball, basketball, or other games from early childhood, very few indeed learn to play the game of science at an early age, if at all. I think this a pity. You don't have to be exceptional to *enjoy* science: very few people become scientists, and even fewer win Nobel prizes, just as very few people become professional baseball players, and only the best ever attain the Hall of Fame.

This little book can show the excitement of the game of science only sporadically and fleetingly. Some day, if you happen to engage in research, you may find yourself in the midst of a scientific controversy. And the difficulty, as always, will be: how to find "stimulating and strategic questions."

Let us, very briefly, look at the things that are not yet understood (obviously, that is the direction from which "stimulating questions" are most likely to come) and see if we can get a hint of what is going to be in store for us in the near future.

The material of Chapters II and III—the physics of frequencies, waves, resonators, and decibels—may seem well-understood, cut-and-dried. In fact, I say as much in Chapter V. Yet acousticians are wrestling with some vexing problems of sound propagation in inhomogeneous media, that is, substances in which the velocity of sound varies from one place to another. There are a great many unanswered questions in underwater acoustics, and in the field of ultrasonics (very high frequency sound) the surface has barely been scratched.

We know much about man's ability to classify, distinguish, and recognize sounds. We have loudness curves, pitch curves, difference limens, and threshold curves. But what do all these things tell us about our ability to recognize the voice of a friend or to understand English spoken with a heavy accent?

It is perhaps unfortunate for the student of hearing that Fourier ever discovered his famous theorem that all sounds, however complicated, can be considered as built up of many simple sine waves. It was only natural that hearing should be investigated with the simplest possible sounds; so almost all our knowledge is based on measurements with sinusoids. What is unfortunate about all this is that sine waves are also the most meaningless sounds that one can think of. The sounds that are meaningful to us—speech, music, traffic noise—are anything but sinusoids, and the belief is rising (from such contradictions to Ohm's Law as we have seen) that the ear is more than an organ to break down complex sounds into sine waves. The ear and brain seem to operate on *patterns* of sound, and ordinarily we are not aware of the constituent sine waves in the pattern. I think that the most exciting and profitable work is going to be done in this field of *pattern recognition*. But how do you go about it? That, you will recognize, is the vital, strategic question, and people are presently working with it, trying to find a stimulating question that may start them on the way.

All is not well, as we have seen, with the understanding of the cochlea. The vexing problems of how the hair cells are stimulated, what role is played by the shearing forces, and how the hair cells eventually stimulate the nerve fibers are of great importance but are as yet almost entirely uncomprehended.

The operation of the nervous system is, without a doubt, one of the very great remaining mysteries of science. We know fairly well how an axon works, we have some glimmerings of knowledge about how dendrites and synapses work; but we know next to nothing about the way nerves interconnect, interplay, perform intricate logical operations, and keep the whole complex human body (including the nervous system itself!) in co-ordination. In my opinion research on the nervous system is going to become one of the major scientific endeavors in years to come. We shall have to study nervous systems of all kinds, from the relative simplicity of the earthworm to the utter complexity of man. We shall have to study the nervous system in real life, physiologically and psychologically, and with mathematical and electronic models.

The phenomena of speech are relatively well understood, but we still do not know precisely how all the various sounds are produced and what distinguishes one from another. What, for instance, makes one person sound distinctly different from another, although both make (as far as we can tell) the same gestures with their vocal apparatus? About the control of speech production by the nervous system we have, again, only rudimentary ideas.

As we have seen on several occasions, our knowledge of animal hearing and sound production is very scant. I think that if we understood the much simpler mechanism in lower animals, we would find it easier to ask good questions about the higher forms and man. As forms of life evolve they acquire more complex and specialized organs, but most of these are built from existing, simpler organs, as, for instance, the ear, which is constructed from the units of the primitive lateral line organ. Certainly we could learn a lot about hair cells from the lateral line organ.

Whichever is the way in which future progress will be made, we can be sure that little by little our understanding of the world we live in will deepen and expand. But we must be prepared to relinquish the cherished old theories we grew up with, as new insight gains ground and new relations are uncovered. This is not always easy; we have been brought up in a society that believes in immutable and unchangeable truths. To accept the fact that in science today's truth may be tomorrow's fallacy goes against the grain of our very culture. It is an astute person, indeed, who can face up to this reality. Perhaps, too, this dilemma between society's demand for absolute truth and science's demand for relative truth makes the scientist the misunderstood figure he is. It certainly looks like a real conflict, but perhaps the solution is not as difficult as it seems. I remember having read, many years ago, a statement by an obscure German philosopher (whose name I have forgotten) which read: "Truth is not eternal; it is a state of affairs." If the state of affairs does not change very much, as in a society where it is fixed by laws and conventions, truth tends to become absolute; in science the state of affairs changes rapidly all the time, and truth is often volatile and short-lived.

SUGGESTED READING

A few of the books in this bibliography have been included for historical reasons. Chiefly, however, each has been chosen from among many worthy alternatives as supplementing or extending work covered in this book. The books cited are not necessarily easy or popular; rather, they are authoritative. They themselves provide numerous references to other works.

H. L. F. von Helmholtz, *Sensations of Tone* (London: Longmans, Green, 1885), 576 pp.
> Helmholtz was a far-ranging intellectual giant of the nineteenth century—a physician, physiologist, philosopher, and theoretical physicist—who discovered the law of conservation of energy. The larger part of his book is devoted to an explanation of music in terms of acoustics and hearing, but the first 150 pages deal with the nature of sound, the analysis of voice sounds into component frequencies, the synthesis of voice sounds out of component frequencies, and the mechanisms of speech and hearing. Many interesting references to contemporary and earlier work are given.

Sir Richard Paget, *Human Speech* (New York: Harcourt, Brace & Co., 1930), 360 pp.

Sir Richard Paget was all one expects of the British amateur scientist. His book is noteworthy for its simple, accurate description of the nature and mechanism of production of speech sounds. The fact that the ideas concerning the origin of language which he advanced in the second half of his book are now judged to be nonsense in no way detracts from the accuracy and value of the first half.

Harvey Fletcher, *Speech and Hearing in Communication* (New York: Van Nostrand, 1953), 461 pp.

Fletcher's book is clear and sensible and reflects a great deal of personal experience in, and personal contribution to, the field of speech and hearing.

S. S. Stevens and Hallowell Davis, *Hearing* (New York: Wiley, 1938), 489 pp.

The psychology and physiology of hearing.

S. S. Stevens, *Handbook of Experimental Psychology* (New York: Wiley, 1951), 1436 pp.

The sections on speech and hearing are noteworthy for their scope, clarity, and succinctness. The book has many valuable sections on other matters as well, such as nerves and the brain.

Hallowell Davis, "Biophysics and Physiology of the Inner Ear," *Physiological Reviews,* Vol. 37, No. 1, January 1957, p. 1.

J. C. R. Licklider, "Auditory Frequency Analysis," p. 253, *Information Theory,* edited by E. C. Cherry (London: Butterworths Scientific Publications, 1956).

R. Galambos, "Neural Mechanisms of Audition," *Physiological Reviews,* 34 (1954), pp. 497–528.

These articles review in detail the up-to-date knowledge of the physiology of hearing. Also included is a goodly measure of auditory theory as well as models of the hearing mechanism.

S. S. Stevens, J. G. C. Loring, and Dorothy Cohen, *Bibliography on Hearing* (Cambridge: Harvard University Press, 1955), 599 pp.

This bibliography, which covers the years 1841–1952, may seem a little frustrating because it directs the reader to so many generally inaccessible sources.

R. K. Potter, G. A. Kopp, and H. C. Green, *Visible Speech* (New York: Van Nostrand, 1947), 441 pp.

The authors of *Visible Speech* have given that name, used earlier by Melville Bell for his pictographic representation of speech sounds, to spectrograms of speech. The book contains many spectrograms and discusses the reading of such records of speech sounds.

Joshua Whatmough, *Language* (New York: St. Martin's Press, 1957), 230 pp.

This little book relates the fascinating story of language and the science of linguistics. It incorporates the thinking of modern researchers concerning the codes of communication.

Colin Cherry, *On Human Communication* (New York: Wiley, 1957), 333 pp.

Cherry's book ranges broadly over the field of human communication. It can serve to introduce the reader to a number of important fields, and especially that variously designated as *information theory* or *communication theory*. An ample bibliography directs the reader to more detailed material.

P. M. Morse, *Vibration and Sound* (New York: McGraw-Hill, 1948), 468 pp.

Physical acoustics for the mathematically inclined.

L. L. Beranek, *Acoustics* (New York: McGraw-Hill, 1954), 481 pp.

Acoustics from the engineering point of view is covered comprehensively. The chapters concerning loudspeakers, loudspeaker enclosures, and horns particularly are worth reading.

The Journal of The Acoustical Society of America, American Institute of Physics, 335 East 45th Street, New York 17, New York.

This monthly journal is available on subscription. Associate membership in the Acoustical Society of America is also available to interested persons and brings them the *Journal*. The *Journal* provides the best access to current work in acoustics, including speech and hearing.

E. Witschi, *Development of Vertebrates* (Philadelphia: Saunders, 1956), 588 pp.

A general text of embryology, treating the development of the ear in more detail than most other textbooks.

Donald R. Griffin, *Listening in the Dark* (New Haven: Yale University Press, 1958), 413 pp.

The absorbing story of echolocation in bats, birds, fishes, and man, written in a lucid and fascinating style.

INDEX

227